# VIKING KNITS

DESIGNS IN COLLABORATION WITH **STRIKKEMEKKA**

LASSE L. MATBERG

# VIKING KNITS

## OVER 40 SCANDI KNITS FOR MEN, WOMEN & CHILDREN

SEARCH PRESS

First published in English in 2023
by Search Press Limited
Wellwood, North Farm Road,
Tunbridge Wells, Kent TN2 3DR

First published in Norwegian in 2021
by Vigmostad & Bjørke
Kanalveien 51, 5068 Bergen, Norway
Copyright © Vigmostad & Bjørken AS, 2021
Published by agreement with Hagen Agency, Oslo

Graphic production: John Grieg, Bergen
Book and cover design: Trine + Kim Designstudio
Cover photo: Heidi Rimereit
Photographs on pages 38, 40, 44, 58, 65, 85 (left), 86, 89, 144 and 147:
Albertine Vestvik
Photographs on pages 22, 126 and 129: Thomas Vaaland
All remaining photographs: Heidi Rimereit
Knitting designs: Strikkemekka (www.strikkemekka.no) and Ber-Lin Design
Many thanks to the models: Synne Domért Gulliksen, Hannah Nilssen Matberg,
Arne Johan Matberg, Elliot Saiti and Lykke Emilie Aase

ISBN: 978-1-80092-077-4
ebook ISBN: 978-1-80093-068-1

**Suppliers**
The yarns in this book are available to buy directly from www.yarnmania.com
If you have difficulty in obtaining any of the materials and equipment mentioned in this
book, then please visit the Search Press website for details of alternative suppliers:
www.searchpress.com

For more information about Lasse Matberg, visit his Instagram: @lasselom

# CONTENTS

# PREFACE

This book is my homage to crafts. I come from a family where making things with our hands has always been important, generation after generation. I myself became fascinated by crafts at an early age, maybe because my dad was a carpenter and I spent a lot of time wearing his carpenter's belt. I also listened wide-eyed to all my grandfather's stories from his long working life as a caretaker, sheet metal worker, plumber and shipbuilder, and the tales he passed down from his father, my great-grandfather, who was a farmer as well as being the village shoemaker. And it was through these stories that I learned, at an early age, that it's good honest work that gets you furthest in life.

I also have lots of childhood memories of my mother and grandmother knitting. In the autumn and winter, I think they knitted practically every evening, making beautiful sweaters, hats, gloves and warm winter socks that the family wore a lot. One of my favourite sweaters, which I still have, was one my mother knitted me. It was brown with a check pattern and a polo neck.

At the time, I didn't think about how much work actually goes went into producing a handmade, knitted sweater. Today I know that knitting is a proud tradition and I'm pleased to help pass it on. I still think a warm, hand-knitted sweater that fits well is one of the best garments you can wear and own. In this book I've brought together my favourite sweaters, with versions for men and women, and for children too. They are comfortable and elegant, whether you are dressing for unpredictable weather, an active day or a mild summer evening.

Several of the sweaters are inspired by the crafts and style of the Vikings. Some are practical and warm, and some are more ornamented and showy. The Vikings did not knit the way we do; they used a technique – now thousands of years old – known as *nålebinding* to make socks and mittens using only one needle. We also know that the Vikings loved colour, as is reflected in the colours of the clothes in this book.

I hope this book will inspire you to create something worthwhile with your hands, giving you a sense of achievement and making you and others happy for many years to come.

*Lasse*

# YARN

All the patterns use one of the three yarns listed below. You can substitute other yarns with similar characteristics but, if you do, it is important to check your tension (gauge).

**Gann Garn – Sky**
62% baby alpaca, 16% acrylic, 22% nylon, 50g (1¾oz) = approx 150m (164yd).

Tension (gauge): 17 sts and 21 rounds to 10cm (4in) using 6mm (UK 4, US 10) needles.
Recommended needle size: 5mm (UK 6, US 8) and 6mm (UK 4, US 10).

A fluffy, super-soft, light and lovely alpaca yarn with a cable-spun core. The surface is gently brushed and the yarn is great for light garments. Sky goes a long way and comes in clear, clean colours as well as beautiful natural shades and pastels. Sky is perfect for cosy sweaters, scarves, loose necklines and accessories.

**Gann Garn – Tweed**
80% wool, 20% polyamide, 50g (1¾oz) = approx 112m (122yd).

Tension (gauge): 17 sts and 24 rounds to 10cm (4in) using 5mm (UK 6, US 8) needles.
Recommended needle size: 5mm (UK 6, US 8).

A classic tweed yarn with a rustic look. The yarn comes in colours ideal for single-colour sweaters and cardigan patterns, Icelandic sweaters and other classic knits, for sport and leisure use, and for accessories. Tweed is great for textured patterns and stocking (stockinette) stitch, brioche and classic Aran cables, and is ideal for adults and children.

**Gann Garn – Myk Merino**
100% superwash merino wool, 50g (1¾oz) = approx 120m (131yd).

Tension (gauge): 22 sts and 28 rounds to 10cm (4in) using 4mm needles (UK 8, US 6).
Recommended needle size: 4mm (UK 8, US 6).

A round-spun yarn in 100% soft, lovely merino wool. This is a superwash yarn, making it especially good for baby clothes and children's knits that may need frequent washing. This yarn is also perfect for cardigans, jackets, sweaters, skirts, jumpers and tops for adults and children. It knits up well, producing even, attractive stitches, making it especially good for cables, textured knits and lace as well as stocking (stockinette) stitch and Fair Isle.

## ABBREVIATIONS

**approx** = approximately

**beg** = begin

**cont** = continue

**dec** = decrease

**dpns** = double-pointed needles

**foll** = follow/following

**inc** = increase

**k** = knit

**k2tog** = knit 2 sts together

**p** = purl

**p2tog** = purl 2 sts together

**patt** = pattern

**psso** = pass slipped stitch over

**rem** = remain/remaining

**rep** = repeat

**sl** = slip

**st/sts** = stitch/stitches

**TBL** = through back loop

**tog** = together

**yo** = yarn over

# THE BEST
# EVERYDAY
# SWEATERS

# LASSE SWEATER

The first time I put it on, it was as if this sweater had chosen me so it simply had to be called the Lasse sweater. It's a big, warm, airy sweater that embraces you like a bear hug.

**YARN**
Gann Garn Sky (62% baby alpaca, 16% acrylic, 22% nylon, 50g (1¾oz) = approx 150m (164yd))

**DIFFICULTY**
Intermediate

**SIZES**
S(M:L:XL:XXL:LASSE)
See garment measurements below to check sizing

**GARMENT MEASUREMENTS**
Chest approx 100(108:116:124:136:124)cm
(39¼(42½:45½:48¾:53½:48¾)in)
Length approx 65(67:69:71:73:76)cm
(25½(26½:27¼:28:28¾:30)in)
Sleeve length approx 55(56:56:57:57:62)cm
(21¾(22:22:22½:22½:24½)in)

**YARN AMOUNT**
10(10:11:12:13:13) balls

**SHADE USED IN VERSIONS SHOWN**
Natural 601
(Alternative colourways: Cognac 604 on page 16 and Light grey 606 on page 17)

**NOTIONS**
Optional: one 22–25mm (¾–1in) diameter button

**SUGGESTED NEEDLES**
5mm (UK 6, US 8) and 6mm (UK 4, US 10) long and short circular needles and dpns. Change from long to short circular needle and to dpns as number of sts and diameter of work decreases and vice versa.

**TENSION (GAUGE)**
18 sts and 22 rounds to approx 10cm (4in) over pattern using 6mm (UK 4, US 10) needles. Remember that you need to maintain an even tension for a successful result. Check your tension by knitting a test swatch. Count the number of stitches per 10cm (4in). If you have more stitches than stated, go up a needle size. If you have fewer stitches, switch to smaller needles.

**BODY**
Cast on 180(196:208:224:244:224) sts using 5mm (UK 6, US 8) circular needle.
Work 6cm (2½in) in k1, p1 rib in the round.
Change to 6mm (UK 4, US 10) circular needles.
Place a marker at each side, marking 91(99:105:113:123:113) sts for front and 89(97:103:111:121:111) sts for back. Cont in patt following chart.
When work measures 43(44:45:46:47:50)cm (17(17¼:17¾:18:18½:19¾)in) from cast on edge, divide and work each side separately, knitting flat.

## BACK

You will have 89(97:103:111:121:111) sts for the back. Work back and forth in patt as set apart from 1 edge st at each side. These edge sts are always knit. At the same time, dec at both sides on alt rows, decreasing 2, 1, 1 sts at armhole edges for all sizes.

When work measures 61(63:64:66:67:70)cm (24(24¾:25¼:26:26½:27½)in) cont in garter stitch patt for shoulders (see instructions on page 15).

When work measures 63(65:67:69:71:74)cm (24¾(25½:26½:27¼:28:29¼)in) cast (bind) off centre 33(35:35:37:37:37) sts for neck. Work each side separately.

Cont back and forth in garter stitch patt as before, at the same time decreasing 1 st at neck edge on every alt row until there are 22(25:28:31:36:31) shoulder sts. When work measures 65(67:69:71:73:76)cm (25½(26½:27¼:28:28¾:30)in), place sts on holder. Work other side the same way, reversing shaping.

## FRONT

You will have 91(99:105:113:123:113) sts for the front. Work back and forth shaping armhole as for back. At the same time, when work measures 2(2:3:3:4:4)cm (¾(¾:1¼:1¼:1½:1½)in) from divide, cast (bind) off centre 19(21:21:23:23:23) sts for V-neck. 32(35:38:41:46:41) sts rem for each side. Work each side of front separately.

### Right front

Break yarn and rejoin at neck edge after cast (bind) off. Cont back and forth in patt as set apart from 1 edge st at each side. At the same time, dec 1 st at neck edge on row 1(1:1:3:3:3). Rep this decrease at neck on every fifth row until you have decreased 9 sts in total. 23(26:29:32:37:32) sts rem. When work measures 61(63:64:66:67:70)cm (24(24¾:25¼:26:26½:27½)in), cont in garter stitch patt for shoulders.

When work measures 65(67:69:71:73:76)cm (25½(26½:27¼:28:28¾:30)in), dec 1 st at neck and place rem 22(25:28:31:36:31) shoulder sts on holder.

### Left front

Work as for right front reversing shaping. Set work aside while you knit the sleeves.

## SLEEVES

Cast on 44(46:46:48:48:48) sts using 5mm (UK 6, US 8) dpns. Work 6cm (2½in) in k1, p1 rib in the round. Change to 6mm (UK 4, US 10) needles. Knit 1 round increasing 8 sts evenly across round to 52(54:54:56:56:56) sts.

Place marker at beg of round = centre underarm. Cont in patt following chart. At the same time, on round 1, inc 1 st each side of marker. Rep increases every 3.5(3:3:2.5:2.5:2.5)cm (1⅜(1¼:1¼:1:1:1)in) until you have worked increases 14(15:16:18:19:19) times in total and there are 80(82:86:90:94:94) sts. When sleeve measures 55(56:56:57:57:62)cm (21¾(22:22:22½:22½:24½)in) or desired length, divide work at marker. Work back and forth in patt as before. At the same time, dec at both sides on alt rows, decreasing 2, 1, 1, sts at armhole edges for all sizes. Cast (bind) off.

Knit other sleeve the same way.

## MAKING UP

Graft or sew together at shoulders.

## SHAWL COLLAR

Beg at right front (RS). Pick up along right side of V-neck, back neck, left side of V-neck: 137(141:141:145:145:145) sts using 5mm (UK 6, US 8) circular needle. Number of sts must be odd. Work 12cm (4¾in) in k1, p1 rib working back and forth. Cast (bind) off loosely in rib.

Overlap ends of collar and sew to front. Add optional decorative button – see photographs on page 16. Graft or sew in sleeves.

## GARTER STITCH PATTERN FOR SHOULDERS:

*Row 1 (RS): knit.
Row 2 (WS): purl.
Row 3 (RS): purl.
Row 4 (WS): knit.*
Rep from * to *.

## CHART

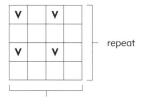

repeat

repeat

☐ = knit (knit on RS, purl on WS)

V = purl (purl on RS, knit on WS)

# POWER SWEATER

A fantastic everyday sweater that gives me an energy boost.
It's close fitting without being tight, and is a comfortable length.
Everyone deserves a Power Sweater.

**YARN**
Gann Garn Tweed (80% wool, 20% polyamide,
50g (1¾oz) = approx 112m (122yd))

**DIFFICULTY**
Intermediate

**SIZES**
S(M:L:XL:XXL:LASSE)
See garment measurements below to check sizing

**GARMENT MEASUREMENTS**
Chest approx 95(102:109:116:124:124)cm
(37½(40¼:43:45½:48¾:48¾)in)
Length approx 66(68:70:72:74:76)cm
(26(26¾:27½:28¼:29¼:30)in)
Sleeve length approx 50(50:52:52:53:53)cm
(19¾(19¾:20½:20½:20¾:20¾)in)

**YARN AMOUNT**
9(10:11:12:13:13) balls

**SHADE USED IN VERSIONS SHOWN**
Grey-brown 911
(Alternative colourway: Dark denim 906, page 21)

**SUGGESTED NEEDLES**
4mm (UK 8, US 6) and 5mm (UK 6, US 8) long and
short circular needles and dpns. Change from long
to short circular needle and to dpns as number of sts
and diameter of work decreases and vice versa.

**TENSION (GAUGE)**
17 sts and 24 rounds to approx 10cm (4in) over stocking
(stockinette) stitch using 5mm (UK 6, US 8) needles.
Remember that you need to maintain an even tension
for a successful result. Check your tension by knitting
a test swatch. Count the number of stitches per 10cm
(4in). If you have more stitches than stated, go up
a needle size. If you have fewer stitches, switch to
smaller needles.

**BODY**
Cast on 162(174:186:198:210:210) sts using 5mm
(UK 6, US 8) circular needle. Place marker at each
side, marking 81(87:93:99:105:105) sts each for front
and back. Work in the round in patt following chart.
Cont until work measures approx 48(49:50:51:52:
53)cm (19(19¼:19¾:20:20½:20¾)in). Cast (bind)
off 12 sts on each side, 6 sts each side of marker. Set
work aside while you knit sleeves.

## SLEEVES

Cast on 36(36:38:38:40:42) sts using 4mm (UK 8, US 6) dpns. Work 6cm (2½in) in k1, p1 rib in the round. Change to 5mm needles (UK 6, US 8) and work 1 round at the same time increasing evenly across round to 45(49:49:51:55:55) sts.

Place marker at beg of round = centre underarm. Count out from centre to determine start of patt and work in the round in patt following chart at the same time increasing 1 st each side of marker approx every 5.5(5.5:5:4.5:4.5:4.5)cm (2¼(2¼:2:1¾:1¾:1¾)in) until there are 61(65:67:71:75:75) sts in total. Work until sleeve measures stated or desired length. Cast (bind) off 12 sts at centre underarm, 6 sts each side of marker. Set aside and work other sleeve the same way.

## YOKE

Place all pieces on the same 5mm (UK 6, US 8) circular needle with one sleeve positioned over each set of cast (bound) off sts on body, placing markers at all four joins. 236(256:272:292:312:312) rem sts. Cont in same patt as before and beg decreasing for raglan: work until 2 sts before marker, sl1 loosely, k1, psso, k2tog. Work raglan decreases at all four joins on every alt round. 8 sts decreased per round. Work raglan decreases 4(5:5:6:7:7) times in total. Now cont decreasing sleeve sts only: dec 1 st on every alt round 16(17:18:19:20:20) times in total while working body sts straight up with no decrease. 9 sts rem for each shoulder. Now decrease only front and back sts (not sleeve sts): work front until 1 st rem (you are now at shoulder), sl1, k1 from shoulder, psso, work 7 sts in patt as before, k2tog. Work decreases in same way on each shoulder/front and shoulder/back on each round. 4 sts decreased per round. After working 9(10:13:14:16:16) rounds of decreases, cast (bind) off centre 25(27:27:29:29:29) sts on front. Work back and forth, decreasing at shoulder as before on each round following patt and now p2tog at shoulders on WS. At the same time, beg to decrease for neck: dec 1 st at beg of each row six times, three times each side of neck, until you have decreased 15(16:19:20:22:22) times at shoulder. Cast (bind) off rem sts.

## NECKBAND

Using 4mm (UK 8, US 6) circular needle, pick up 86(86:90:90:96:96) sts around neck. Work 3cm (1¼in) in k1, p1 rib in the round. Purl 1 round (forms foldline). Work 3cm (1¼in) k1, p1 rib in the round. Cast (bind) off loosely in rib. Fold edge to WS and sew down loosely.

## MAKING UP

Sew together at underarms. Weave in all loose ends on WS.

Wash sweater and stretch into shape while lying flat to dry. Gently press on WS if desired.

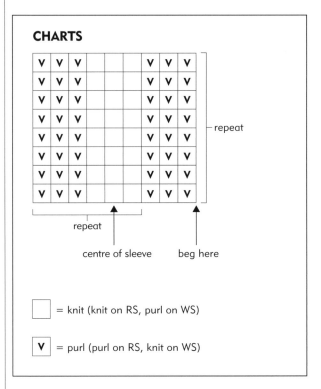

### CHARTS

repeat

repeat

centre of sleeve     beg here

☐ = knit (knit on RS, purl on WS)

V = purl (purl on RS, knit on WS)

# SYNNE SWEATER
## WOMEN

A great, colourful sweater in a Nordic pattern that's sure to catch the eye.

**YARN**
Gann Garn Sky (62% baby alpaca, 16% acrylic, 22% nylon, 50g (1¾oz) = approx 150m (164yd))

**DIFFICULTY**
Experienced

**SIZES**
S(M:L:XL:XXL)
See garment measurements below to check sizing

**GARMENT MEASUREMENTS**
Chest approx 95(105:112:124:133)cm
(37½(41½:44:48¾:52¼)in)
Length approx 61(63:65:67:69)cm
(24(24¾:25½:26½:27¼)in)
Sleeve length approx 45(46:46:47:47)cm
(17¾(18:18:18½:18½)in)

**YARN AMOUNT**
Yarn A: 6(6:7:7:8) balls
Yarn B: 1(1:1:2:2) balls
Yarn C: 2(2:2:2:2) balls

**SHADES USED IN VERSION SHOWN**
Yarn A: Dark moss green 611
Yarn B: Cognac 604
Yarn C: Light grey 606

**SUGGESTED NEEDLES**
5mm (UK 6, US 8) and 6mm (UK 4, US 10) long and short circular needles and dpns. Change from long to short circular needle and to dpns as number of sts and diameter of work decreases and vice versa.

> **TIP:** The tension will be tighter when working the Fair Isle pattern and it is often useful to go up 0.5mm or 1mm in needle size (one or two UK/US sizes).

**TENSION (GAUGE)**
17 sts and 21 rounds to approx 10cm (4in) over stocking (stockinette) stitch using 6mm (UK 4, US 10) needles. Remember that you need to maintain an even tension for a successful result. Check your tension by knitting a test swatch. Count the number of stitches per 10cm (4in). If you have more stitches than stated, go up a needle size. If you have fewer stitches, switch to smaller needles.

> **TIP:** To ensure a good result when knitting with two or more colours, always hold yarns in the same position behind the work. Decide to keep the background colour innermost and the contrast colour outermost, for example.

## BODY

Cast on 162(178:190:210:226) sts using 5mm
(UK 6, US 8) circular needle and yarn A. Work
5cm (2in) in twisted rib (k1TBL, p1) in the round
for all sizes. Change to 6mm (UK 4, US 10)
needle. Place marker at each side, marking
81(89:95:105:113) sts each for front and back.
Work in stocking (stockinette) stitch in the round
until work measures approx 41(42:43:44:45)cm
(16¼(16½:17:17¼:17¾)in). At the same time, on last
round cast (bind) off 10 sts at each side for armhole,
5 sts on each side of each marker. Set work aside
while you knit sleeves.

## SLEEVES

Cast on 32(34:36:38:40) sts using 5mm (UK 6, US 8)
dpns and yarn A. Work 5cm (2in) in twisted rib in the
round as for bottom of body. Change to 6mm needles
(UK 4, US 10) and knit 1 round increasing 3(5:7:7:7)
sts evenly across round to 35(39:43:45:47) sts. Place
marker at beg of round = centre underarm.
Count out from centre sleeve to check where round
starts on chart and work pattern A. Then cont in
stocking (stockinette) stitch using yarn A. At the same
time, inc 1 st each side of marker on first round. Rep
increases approx every 3cm (1¼in) in all sizes until you
have worked increases 13(13:13:13:14) times in total.
61(65:69:71:75) rem sts.
Work until sleeve measures 45(46:46:47:47)cm
(17¾(18:18:18½:18½)in) or desired length, and on
last round cast (bind) off 10 sts at centre underarm,
5 sts each side of marker.
Set work aside and work other sleeve the same way.

## YOKE

Place all pieces on the same 6mm (UK 4,
US 10) circular needle with one sleeve
positioned over each set of cast (bound) off sts
on body. 244(268:288:312:336) sts. Beg at back
at right shoulder. Knit 1 round using yarn A
decreasing 4(4:0:0:0) sts evenly across round.
240(264:288:312:336) rem sts. Work pattern B

and then work pattern C, decreasing as shown in
charts, opposite.
80(88:96:104:112) rem sts. Knit 1 round
decreasing 0(4:8:12:16) sts evenly across round to
80(84:88:92:96) sts.

## NECKBAND

Change to 5mm (UK 6, US 8) circular needle. Work
from WS or turn work so WS faces outwards.
Work twisted rib (k1TBL, p1) in the round using yarn
C until neck measures 16cm (6in). Cast (bind) off
loosely in rib. Fold neck over to RS.

## MAKING UP

Graft or sew together at underarms.

# CHARTS

**PATTERN A**

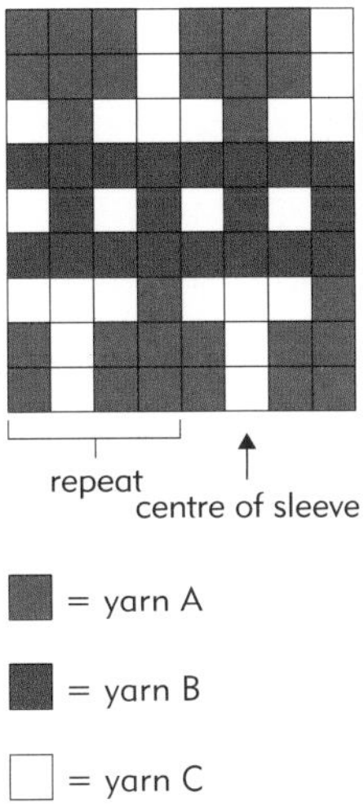

repeat

centre of sleeve

■ = yarn A

■ = yarn B

☐ = yarn C

**PATTERN B**

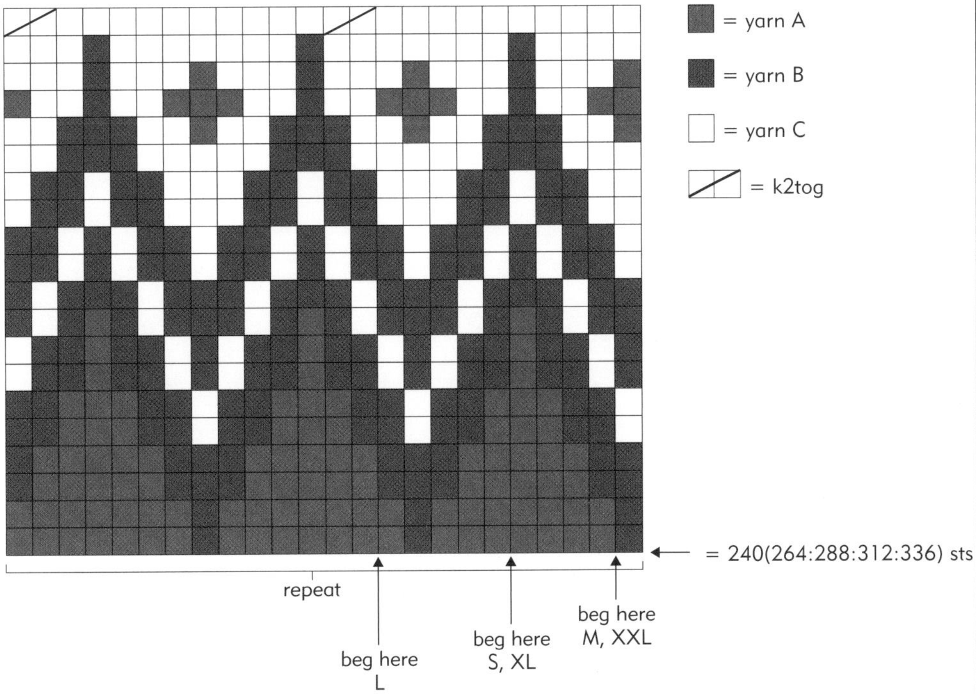

■ = yarn A

■ = yarn B

☐ = yarn C

⧄ = k2tog

= 240(264:288:312:336) sts

repeat

beg here
L

beg here
S, XL

beg here
M, XXL

**PATTERN C**

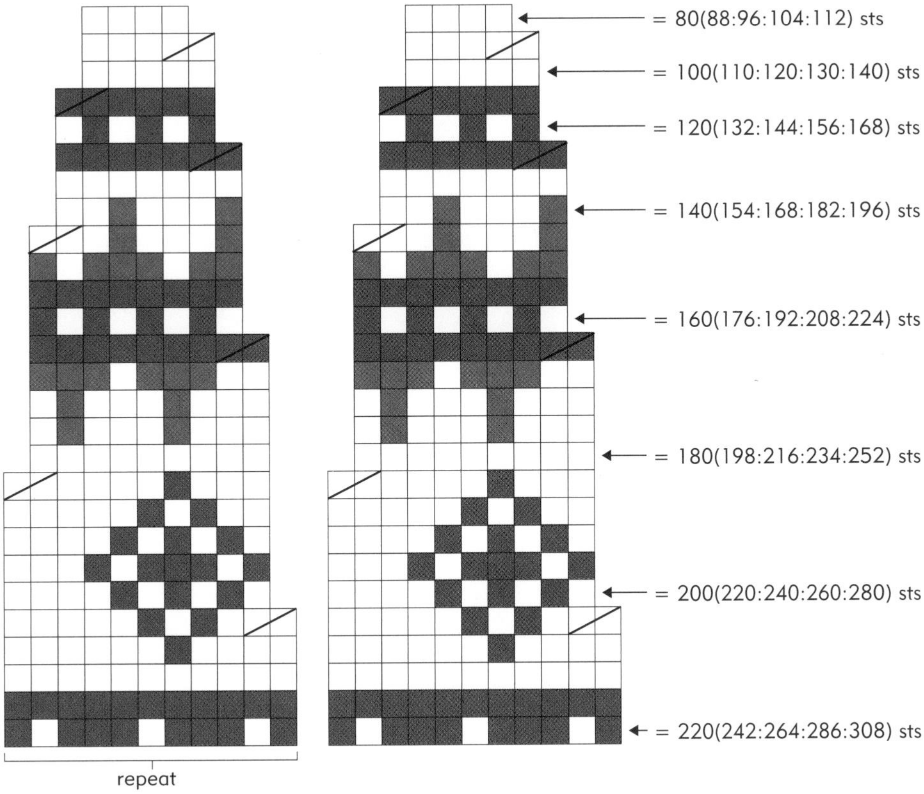

= 80(88:96:104:112) sts

= 100(110:120:130:140) sts

= 120(132:144:156:168) sts

= 140(154:168:182:196) sts

= 160(176:192:208:224) sts

= 180(198:216:234:252) sts

= 200(220:240:260:280) sts

= 220(242:264:286:308) sts

repeat

# FIABA SWEATER
## WOMEN

*Fiaba* is Italian for adventure. This is a stylish sweater in moss stitch made with a soft alpaca yarn for people with a love of adventure.

**YARN**
Gann Garn Sky (62% baby alpaca, 16% acrylic, 22% nylon, 50g (1¾oz) = approx 150m (164yd))

**DIFFICULTY**
Beginner

**SIZES**
XS(S:M:L:XL:XXL)
See garment measurements to check sizing

**GARMENT MEASUREMENTS**
Chest approx 89(98:106:115:122:134)cm (35(38½:41¾:45¼:48:52¾)in)
Length approx 56(58:60:62:64:66)cm (22(22¾:23½:24½:25¼:26)in)
Sleeve length approx 48cm (19in) or desired length

**YARN AMOUNT**
Yarn A: 9(9:10:10:11:11) balls
Yarn B: one ball for all sizes

**SHADES USED IN VERSION SHOWN**
Yarn A: Light beige 605
Yarn B: Cognac 604

**SUGGESTED NEEDLES**
5mm (UK 6, US 8) and 6mm (UK 4, US 10) long and short circular needles and dpns. Change from long to short circular needle and to dpns as number of sts and diameter of work decreases and vice versa.

**TENSION (GAUGE)**
17 sts and 21 rounds to approx 10cm (4in) over stocking (stockinette) stitch using 6mm (UK 4, US 10) needles. Remember that you need to maintain an even tension for a successful result. Check your tension by knitting a test swatch. Count the number of stitches per 10cm (4in). If you have more stitches than stated, go up a needle size. If you have fewer stitches, switch to smaller needles.

**BODY**
Cast on 152(168:180:196:208:228) sts using 5mm (UK 6, US 8) circular needle and yarn A. Work k2, p2 rib in the round until work measures approx 6cm (2½in) for all sizes. Change to 6mm (UK 4, US 10) needle. Place marker at each side, marking 77(85:91:99:105:115) sts for front and 75(83:89:97:103:113) sts for back. Work in the round in moss stitch as shown in chart until work measures approx 10(9:10:9:10:9)cm (4(3½:4:3½:4:3½)in). Work stripe patt at the same time cont moss stitch as before. Then work 9(10:10:11:11:12)cm (3½(4:4:4¼:4¼:4¾)in) in moss stitch using yarn A, work stripe patt in moss stitch, then work 9(10:10:11:11:12)cm (3½(4:4:4¼:4¼:4¾)in) in moss stitch using yarn A.

End with stripe patt in moss stitch. Work should now measure approx 36(37:38:39:40:41)cm (14¼(14½:15:15¼:15¾:16¼)in). On last round cast (bind) off 10 sts at each side, 5 sts each side of marker. Set work aside while you knit sleeves.

## SLEEVES
Cast on 32(36:36:36:40:40) sts using 5mm (UK 6, US 8) dpns and yarn A. Work 6cm (2½in) k2, p2 rib in the round. Change to 6mm (UK 4, US 10) needles. Work 1 round using yarn A, increasing evenly across round to 43(45:47:51:53:55) sts.
Place marker at beg of round = centre underarm. Work in moss stitch in the round while increasing 1 st each side of marker approx every 4(4:3.5:3.5:3.5:3.5)cm (1½(1½:1⅜:1⅜:1⅜:1⅜)in) until there are 63(65:69:73:75:79) sts in total. Work until sleeve measures approx 3cm (1¼in) less than total length stated or desired length. Work stripe patt in moss stitch. Cast (bind) off 10 sts at centre underarm, 5 sts each side of marker. Set aside and work other sleeve the same way.

## YOKE
Place all pieces on the same 6mm (UK 4, US 10) circular needle with one sleeve positioned over each set of cast (bound) off sts on body. Place marker at all four joins. 238(258:278:302:318:346) sts. Cont working in the round in moss stitch as before using yarn A. At the same time, on round 1 of yoke, work raglan decrease at all 4 markers: work until 2 sts before marker, sl2 loosely together (as if knitting 2 sts together), k1, pass 2 slipped sts over. Rep raglan decrease at all four joins. 8 sts decreased per round. Dec in the same way on alt rounds until you have worked raglan decreases 15(17:19:22:24:27) times in total. On alt rounds without decreases, work the raglan stitch as a knit stitch. Cast (bind) off centre 15(19:21:23:25:29) sts on front for neck. Work to end of round.
Break yarn and beg at front after cast (bound) off sts. Beg with RS row, decreasing for raglan. Work back

and forth in moss stitch decreasing on every alt row as follows: 3, 2, 2, 1 sts at each side of neck edge in all sizes. Cont until you have worked 19(21:23:26:28:31) raglan decreases on back in total. 59(59:61:59:57:57) rem sts. Work neckband.

## NECKBAND
Move rem sts to 4mm (UK 8, US 6) circular needle and pick up 21(25:27:33:35:35) sts from front neck using yarn A. 80(84:88:92:92:92) sts. Work in k2, p2 rib until neckband measures approx 6cm (2½in). Cast (bind) off loosely in rib. Fold edge to WS and sew down loosely.

## MAKING UP
Sew together at underarms. Weave in all loose ends on WS.

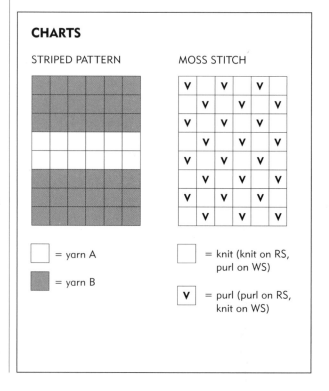

**CHARTS**

STRIPED PATTERN

MOSS STITCH

☐ = yarn A

▨ = yarn B

☐ = knit (knit on RS, purl on WS)

v = purl (purl on RS, knit on WS)

# KNITS FOR THE GREAT OUTDOORS

# SPARK JACKET

A classic, timeless knitted jacket made in a light yarn for breezy summer weather and warm winter days.

## YARN
Gann Garn Myk Merino (100% superwash merino wool, 50g (1¾oz) = approx 120m (131yd))

## DIFFICULTY
Experienced

## SIZES
S(M:L:XL:XXL:LASSE)
See garment measurements below to check sizing

## GARMENT MEASUREMENTS
Chest approx 98(109:116:123:134:134)cm
(38½(43:45½:48½:52¾:52¾)in)
Length approx 66(68:70:72:74:78)cm
(26(26¾:27½:28¼:29¼:30¾)in)
Sleeve length approx 50(50:52:52:53:53)cm
(19¾(19¾:20½:20½:20¾:20¾)in)

## YARN AMOUNT
Yarn A: 9(9:10:10:11:11) balls
Yarn B: 6(6:7:7:8:8) balls

## SHADES USED IN VERSION SHOWN
Yarn A: Natural 701
Yarn B: Petrol 714

## SUGGESTED NEEDLES
3.5mm (UK 9/10, US 4) and 4.5mm (UK 7, US 7) long and short circular needles and dpns. Change from long to short circular needle and to dpns as number of sts and diameter of work decreases and vice versa.

## NOTIONS
8(8:8:9:9:9) 20–25mm (¾–1in) diameter buttons

## TENSION (GAUGE)
22 sts and 27 rounds to approx 10cm (4in) over stocking (stockinette) stitch on 4.5mm (UK 7, US 7) needles. Remember that you need to maintain an even tension for a successful result. Check your tension by knitting a test swatch. Count the number of stitches per 10cm (4in). If you have more stitches than stated, go up a needle size. If you have fewer stitches, switch to smaller needles.

## BODY
Cast on 229(253:269:285:309:309) sts using 3.5mm (UK 9/10, US 4) circular needle and yarn B. Work back and forth in k1, p1 rib. After approx 2cm (¾in), work first buttonhole on right front band by casting (binding) off 2 sts 3 sts from edge. On the following row, cast on 2 sts to replace these. Work until rib measures approx 4cm (1½in) for all sizes. Place the first 10 sts and last 10 sts on a holder. These are for

the front bands which are worked at the end.
209(233:249:265:289:289) rem sts.

Change to 4.5mm (UK 7, US 7) circular needle. Place marker at each side, marking 51(57:61:69:71:71) sts for each front and 107(119:127:135:147:147) sts for back. Work in the round in stocking (stockinette) stitch following patt as shown in chart. Cast on 5 sts at end of round and purl these using yarn A on every round. These will form the steek. Cont until work measures approx 47(48:49:50:51:55)cm (18½(19:19¼:19¾:20: 21¾)in). Cast (bind) off 16 sts on each side, 8 sts each side of marker. Set aside while you work sleeves.

### SLEEVES

Cast on 48(48:52:52:56:56) sts using 3.5mm (UK 9/10, US 4) dpns and yarn B. Work 4cm (1½in) in k1, p1 rib in the round. Change to 4.5mm (UK 7, US 7) needles and work 1 round increasing evenly across round to 63(65:67:71:73:73) sts.

Place marker at beg of round = centre underarm. Work in the round following patt as shown in chart at the same time increasing 1 st each side of marker approx every 4.5(3.5:3.5:3.5:3.5:3.5)cm (1¾(1⅜:1⅜:1⅛:1⅜:1⅜)in) until there are 83(89:93: 97:101:101) sts in total. Work until sleeve measures stated or desired length. End with same round of chart as for body. Cast (bind) off 16 sts at centre underarm, 8 sts each side of marker. Set aside and work other sleeve the same way.

### YOKE

Place all pieces on the same 4.5mm circular needle (UK 7, US 7) with one sleeve positioned over each set of cast (bound)off sts on body = 311(347:371:395:427:427) sts not including the 5 steek sts. Place markers at all four joins. Cont in same patt as before and decrease for raglan using yarn A: work until 3 sts before marker, sl1 loosely, k1, psso, k2, k2tog. Dec at all four joins. 8 sts decreased per round. Dec in the same way on every alt round until you have worked raglan decrease round

21(24:26:29:31:31) times in total. Cast (bind) off centre 19(25:29:31:39:39) sts on front for neck (Note: this number does not include the 5 steek sts). Work to end of round. Break yarn and beg from centre front at neck. Check that you are starting raglan decreases on RS. Work back and forth in patt continuing raglan decreases and continuing to decrease for neck at both sides on every alt row as follows: 4, 3, 2, 1 sts. 64(70:74:72:80:80) rem sts. Set aside while you work front bands.

### MAKING UP

Press cardigan carefully on WS. Using a sewing machine, sew two seams along centre front with smallest zigzag stitch setting. Cut between seams. Sew a seam over the cut edge using normal zigzag stitch.

## FRONT BANDS

Work left front band first. Place the 10 set aside stitches without a buttonhole on a 3.5mm (UK 9/10, US 4) needle. Cast on 5 new sts in towards body and work these in stocking (stockinette) stitch throughout. These 5 sts will form a facing. Work back and forth in rib using yarn B as before until band is long enough to reach stitches at neck edge (stretch band slightly while measuring). Cast (bind) off facing and place band sts on a holder.

Place markers for 8(8:8:9:9:9) buttons. The first buttonhole is already worked, the last button will be in the centre of the neckband and the others should be evenly spaced between them.

Work right band in the same way but making buttonholes to match button markers on left front band.

## NECKBAND

Beg at right front edge. Work sts from right front band on to 3.5mm (UK 9/10, US 4) circular needle using yarn B and work in rib as before. Pick up approx 16(21:25:27:29:29) sts along the cast (bound) off sts for the right neck, knit the set aside neck sts in stocking (stockinette) stitch, pick up the same number of sts for left front neck as for right front neck and work sts from holder for left front band. 117(131:143:147:157) sts. Work back and forth in k1, p1 rib until neck measures approx 3cm (1¼in). NOTE: Remember to work the last buttonhole in right front band. Cast (bind) off the first 10 and last 10 sts for the front bands. Purl 1 row from RS (forms foldline). Work 3cm (1¼in) in k1, p1 rib. Cast (bind) off loosely in rib.

## MAKING UP

Attach front bands and sew down facing on WS. Fold neck edge over to WS and sew down loosely. Sew together at underarms. Weave in all loose ends on WS. Sew on buttons.

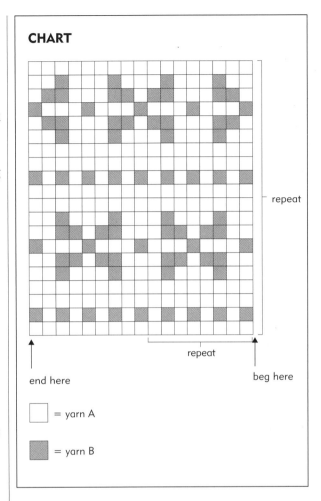

**CHART**

repeat

repeat

end here

beg here

☐ = yarn A

▨ = yarn B

# SPARK SWEATER
## WOMEN

The women's spark sweater is alight with the glow of a setting sun beside a mountain hut. It is knitted in the same comfortable yarn as the men's jacket (see page 36).

**YARN**
Gann Garn Myk Merino (100% superwash merino wool, 50g (1¾oz) = approx 120m (131yd))

**DIFFICULTY**
Intermediate

**SIZES**
XS(S:M:L:XL:XXL)
See garment measurements below to check sizing

**GARMENT MEASUREMENTS**
Chest approx 84(95:102:109:120:130)cm
(33(37½:40¼:43:47¼:51)in)
Length approx 56(58:60:62:64:66)cm
(22(22¾:23½:24½:25¼:26)in)
Sleeve length approx 48cm (19in) or desired length

**YARN AMOUNT**
Yarn A: 7(8:8:9:10:11) balls
Yarn B: 3(4:4:4:5:5) balls

**SHADES USED IN VERSION SHOWN**
Yarn A: Ochre 718
Yarn B: Natural 701

**SUGGESTED NEEDLES**
3.5mm (UK 9/10, US 4) and 4.5mm (UK 7, US 7) long and short circular needles and dpns. Change from long to short circular needle and to dpns as number of sts and diameter of work decreases and vice versa.

**TIP:** To ensure a good result when knitting with two or more colours, always hold yarns in the same position behind the work. Decide to keep the background colour innermost and the contrast colour outermost, for example.

**TENSION (GAUGE)**
22 sts and 28 rounds to approx 10cm (4in) over stocking (stockinette) stitch using 4.5mm (UK 7, US 7) needles. Remember that you need to maintain an even tension for a successful result. Check your tension by knitting a test swatch. Count the number of stitches per 10cm (4in). If you have more stitches than stated, go up a needle size. If you have fewer stitches, switch to smaller needles.

## BODY

Cast on 184(208:224:240:264:288) sts using 3.5mm (UK 9/10, US 4) circular needle and yarn A. Work approx 6cm (2½in) in twisted rib (k1TBL, p1) in the round for all sizes. Change to 4.5mm circular needle (UK 7, US 7). Place marker at each side, marking 93(105:113:121:133:143) sts for front and 91(103:111:119:131:143) sts for back. Work in the round in patt following chart. Cont until work measures approx 37(38:39:40:41:42)cm (14½(15:15¼:15¾:16¼:16½)in). Cast (bind) off 12 sts on each side, 6 sts each side of marker. Set aside while you work sleeves.

## SLEEVES

Cast on 44(46:48:50:52:52) sts using 3.5mm (UK 9/10, US 4) dpns and yarn A. Work 6cm (2½in) in twisted rib (k1TBL, p1) in the round. Change to 4.5mm (UK 7, US 7) needles and knit 1 round increasing evenly across round to 53(57:59:63:67:71) sts. Place marker at beg of round = centre underarm. Count out from centre to determine start of patt and work in the round in patt following chart at the same time as increasing 1 st each side of marker approx every 3.5(3.5:3.5:3.5:3:3)cm (1⅜(1⅜:1⅜:1⅜:1¼:1¼)in) until there are 75(79:83:87:93:97) sts. Work until sleeve measures stated or desired length. Make sure to end with same round of chart as for body. On last round, cast (bind) off 12 sts at centre underarm, 6 sts each side of marker. Set work aside and work other sleeve the same way.

## YOKE

Place all pieces on the same 4.5mm (UK 7, US 7) circular needle with one sleeve positioned over each set of cast (bound) off sts on body. 286(318:342:366:402:434) sts. Mark 1 st at each join, placing markers in first st counting from body. Cont in patt as before, working decreases at all four joins. Always decrease using yarn A. Work until 2 sts before marked st, k2tog, k1, k2togTBL. 8 sts decreased. Dec in the same way on every alt round until you have worked raglan decrease round 20(22:24:27:29:31) times in total. On next round, cast (bind) off centre 11(19:23:27:33:41) sts on front for neck. Work to end of round. Break yarn and beg at front after cast (bound) off sts. Check that you are starting raglan decreases on RS. Work back and forth in patt continuing raglan decreases and decrease at each side of neck on every alt row as follows: 4, 2, 2, 1 sts.

Cont until you have worked 25(27:29:31:34:36) raglan decreases on back in total. 59(63:69:73:79:87) rem sts. Work neckband.

**NECKBAND**

Move rem sts to 3.5mm (UK 9/10, US 4) circular needle and pick up 33(33:35:39:41:41) sts from front neck using yarn A. Approx 92(96:104:112:120:128) sts. Cont in twisted rib, (k1TBL, p1) in the round until neckband measures approx 6cm (2½in). Cast (bind) off loosely in rib. Fold neck edge over to WS and sew down loosely.

**MAKING UP**

Sew together at underarms. Weave in all loose ends on WS.

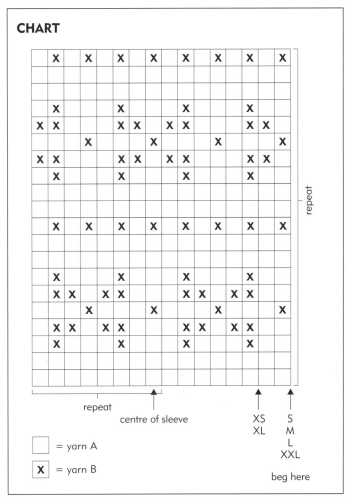

# SPARK SWEATER
## CHILDREN

**YARN**
Gann Garn Myk Merino (100% superwash
merino wool, 50g (1¾oz) = approx 120m (131yd))

**DIFFICULTY**
Intermediate

**SIZES**
Age 2(4:6:8:10:12)
See garment measurements below to check sizing

**GARMENT MEASUREMENTS**
Chest approx 62(65:69:73:76:84)cm
(24½(25½:27¼:28¾:30:33)in
Length approx 37(40:44:48:52:56)cm
(14½(15¾:17¼:19:20½:22)in)
Sleeve length approx 24(27:33:36:38:40)cm
(9½(10¾:13:14¼:15:15¾)in)

**YARN AMOUNT**
Yarn A: 4(4:5:5:6:7) balls
Yarn B: 2(2:2:3:3:4) balls

**SHADES USED IN VERSIONS SHOWN**
Yarn A: Natural 701
Yarn B: Caramel 704
(Alternative colourway: Ochre 718 and Natural 701,
page 47)

**SUGGESTED NEEDLES**
3.5mm (UK 9/10, US 4) and 4.5mm (UK 7, US 7)
long and short circular needles and dpns. Change
from long to short circular needle and to dpns as
number of sts and diameter of work decreases and
vice versa.

> **TIP:** To ensure a good result when knitting with
> two or more colours, always hold yarns in the
> same position behind the work. Decide to keep
> the background colour innermost and the contrast
> colour outermost, for example.

**TENSION (GAUGE)**
22 sts and 28 rounds to approx 10cm (4in) over stocking
(stockinette) stitch using 4.5mm (UK 7, US 7) needles.
Remember that you need to maintain an even tension
for a successful result. Check your tension by knitting
a test swatch. Count the number of stitches per 10cm
(4in). If you have more stitches than stated, go up
a needle size. If you have fewer stitches, switch to
smaller needles.
Most people knit more tightly with Fair Isle than they
do when knitting ordinary stocking (stockinette)
stitch. This means it's a good idea to pay extra
attention to your tension and possibly go up 0.5mm
or 1mm in needle size (1 or 2 UK/US sizes).

## BODY

Cast on 136(144:152:160:168:184) sts using 3.5mm (UK 9/10, US 4) circular needle and yarn A. Work twisted rib (k1TBL, p1) in the round for approx 3(3:3:4:4:4)cm (1¼(1¼:1¼:1½:1½:1½)in). Change to 4.5mm (UK 7, US 7) circular needle. Place marker at each side, marking 69(73:77:81:85:93) sts for front and 67(71:75:79:83:91) sts for back. Work in the round in patt following chart. Cont until work measures approx 25(27:30:33:36:39)cm (9¾(10¾:11¾:13:14¼:15¼)in). Cast (bind) off 10 sts on each side, 5 sts each side of marker. Set aside while you knit sleeves.

## SLEEVES

Cast on 28(32:36:40:40:44) sts using 3.5mm (UK 9/10, US 4) dpns and yarn A. Work twisted rib (k1TBL, p1) in the round for approx 3(3:3:4:4:4)cm (1¼(1¼:1¼:1½:1½:1½)in) as for body. Change to 4.5mm (UK 7, US 7) needles and knit 1 round increasing evenly across round to 45(49:53:57:61:67) sts. Place marker at beg of round = centre underarm. Count out from centre to determine start of patt and work in the round in patt following chart. Note that the pattern will not necessarily match at underarms. Work patt until work measures stated or desired length. Make sure to end with same round of chart as for body. On last round, cast (bind) off 10 sts at centre underarm, 5 sts each side of marker. Set aside and work other sleeve the same way.

## YOKE

Place all pieces on the same 4.5mm (UK 7, US 7) circular needle with one sleeve positioned over each set of cast (bound) off sts on body. 186(202:218:234:250:278) sts. Mark 1 st at each join, placing markers in first st counting from body. 4 sts marked in round. Cont in patt as set, working decreases in same way at all four joins. Always decrease using yarn A. Work until 2 sts before

marked st, sl1 loosely, k1, psso, k1 (marked st), k2tog. 8 sts decreased. Dec on every alt round until you have worked raglan decrease round 11(13:15:16:18:22) times in total. On next round, cast (bind) off centre 19(19:19:21:21:25) sts on front for neck. Work to end of round. Break yarn and beg at front after cast (bound) off sts. Check that you are starting raglan decreases on RS. Work back and forth in patt continuing raglan decreases and decreasing at each side of neck on alt rows as foll: 3, 2 sts for all sizes. Cont until you have worked 14(16:18:19:21:23) raglan decreases on back in total. 45(45:45:51:51:59) rem sts. Work neckband.

## NECKBAND

Pick up sts round neck on 3.5mm (UK 9/10, US 4) needles and knit using yarn A. Pick up 27(27:31:35:35:37) sts from front neck. 72(72:76:86:86:96) rem sts. Cont in twisted rib (k1TBL, p1) in the round until neckband measures approx 5(5:5:6:6:6)cm (2(2:2:2½:2½:2½)in). Cast (bind) off loosely in rib. Fold neck edge over to WS and sew down loosely.

## MAKING UP

Sew together at underarms. Weave in all loose ends neatly on WS.

## CHART

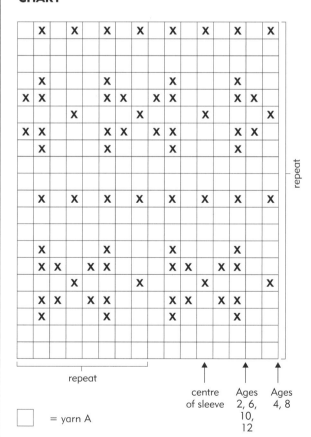

# HEART SWEATER

This sweater is heart-warming in every sense, partly because the pattern looks like little hearts and partly because it's good and warm.

## YARN
Gann Garn Sky (62% baby alpaca, 16% acrylic, 22% nylon, 50g (1¾oz) = approx 150m (164yd))

## DIFFICULTY
Experienced

## SIZES
S(M:L:XL:XXL:LASSE)
See garment measurements below to check sizing

## GARMENT MEASUREMENTS
Chest approx 100(110:120:130:140:130)cm
(39¼(43¼:47¼:51:55¼:51)in)
Length approx 66(68:70:72:74:76)cm
(26(26¾:27½:28¼:29¼:30)in)
Sleeve length approx 50(50:52:52:53:53)cm
(19¾(19¾:20½:20½:20¾:20¾)in)

## YARN AMOUNT
Yarn A: 7(8:8:9:10:9) balls
Yarn B: 2(2:2:2:2:2) balls

## SHADES USED IN VERSION SHOWN
Yarn A: Dark moss green 611
Yarn B: Natural 601

## SUGGESTED NEEDLES
5mm (UK 6, US 8) and 6mm (UK 4, US 10) long and short circular needles and dpns. Change from long to short circular needle and to dpns as number of sts and diameter of work decreases and vice versa.

> **TIP:** To ensure a good result when knitting with two or more colours, always hold yarns in the same position behind the work. Decide to keep the background colour innermost and the contrast colour outermost, for example.

## TENSION (GAUGE)
17 sts and 21 rounds to approx 10cm (4in) over stocking (stockinette) stitch using 6mm (UK 4, US 10) needles. Remember that you need to maintain an even tension for a successful result. Check your tension by knitting a test swatch. Count the number of stitches per 10cm (4in). If you have more stitches than stated, go up a needle size. If you have fewer stitches, switch to smaller needles.

## BODY
Cast on 168(188:204:220:236:220) sts using 5mm (UK 6, US 8) circular needle and yarn A. Work approx 6cm (2½in) in k2, p2 rib in the round for all sizes. Change to 6mm (UK 4, US 10) needle. Place marker at each side, marking 85(95:103:111:119:111) sts for front and 83(93:101:109:117:109) sts for back.

Work in the round in patt following chart. Cont until work measures approx 46(47:48:49:50:51)cm (18(18½:19:19¼:19¾:20)in). Cast (bind) off 12 sts on each side, 6 sts each side of marker. Set aside while you knit sleeves.

### SLEEVES
Cast on 36(36:36:40:40:40) sts on 5mm (UK 6, US 8) dpns using yarn A. Work 6cm (2½in) in k2, p2 rib in the round. Change to 6mm (UK 4, US 10) needles and knit 1 round increasing evenly across round to 47(49:53:55:57:59) sts. Place marker at beg of round = centre underarm. Count out from centre to determine start of patt and work in the round in patt following chart at the same time increasing 1 st each side of marker approx every 4.5(4:4:3.5:3.5:3.5)cm (1¾(1½:1½:1⅜:1⅜:1⅜)in) until there are 67(71:75:79:81:85) sts. Work until sleeve measures stated or desired length. Make sure to end with same round of chart as for body. Cast (bind) off 12 sts at centre underarm, 6 sts each side of marker. Set aside and work other sleeve the same way.

### YOKE
Place all pieces on the same 6mm (UK 4, US 10) circular needle with one sleeve positioned over each set of cast (bound) off sts on body. 254(282:306:330:350:342) sts. At the same time mark 1 st at each join, placing markers in first st counting from body. 4 sts marked in round. Always decrease using yarn A. Work until 2 sts before marked st, sl1 loosely, k1, psso, k1 (marked st), k2tog. Work decreases in same way at all four joins. 8 sts decreased in round. Work in the round in patt as before. Dec in the same way on every alt round until you have worked raglan decrease round 17(19:22:24:26:26) times in total. Cast (bind) off centre 17(23:25:29:33:25) sts on front for neck. Work to end of round. Break yarn and beg at front after cast (bound) off sts. Check that you are starting raglan decreases on RS. Work back and forth in patt, continuing to decrease for raglan and decreasing

for neck at each side of neck edge on alt rows as foll: 3, 2, 1 sts in all sizes. Cont until you have worked 21(23:26:28:30:30) raglan decreases on back in total. 57(63:61:65:65:65) rem sts. Work neckband.

### NECKBAND
Move rem sts to 5mm (UK 6, US 8) circular needle and using yarn A, pick up 23(25:27:31:35:31) sts at front neck. Approx 80(88:88:96:100:96) sts. Cont in k2, p2 rib in the round until neckband measures approx 3cm (1¼in). Purl 1 round (forms foldline). Work 3cm (1¼in) in rib. Cast (bind) off loosely in rib. Fold neck edge over to WS and sew down loosely.

### MAKING UP
Sew together at underarms. Weave in all loose ends on WS.

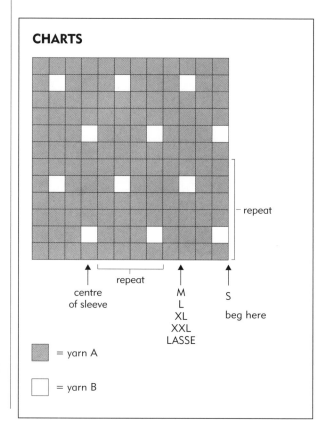

CHARTS

repeat

repeat

centre
of sleeve

M
L
XL
XXL
LASSE

S

beg here

= yarn A

= yarn B

# MOUNTAINTOP SWEATER

This is an impressively beautiful, decorated sweater with a slim-fit style. You'll be dapper, whether you're out and about in town, hiking or out on the slopes.

## YARN
Gann Garn Myk Merino (100% superwash merino wool, 50g (1¾oz) = approx 120m (131yd))

## DIFFICULTY
Experienced

## SIZES
S(M:L:XL:XXL:LASSE)
See garment measurements to check sizing

## GARMENT MEASUREMENTS
Chest approx 95(103:110:118:128:128)cm (37½(40½:43¼:46½:50:50)in)
Length approx 66(68:70:72:74:76)cm (26(26¾:27½:28¼:29¼:30)in)
Sleeve length approx 50(50:52:52:53:53)cm (19¾(19¾:20½:20½:20¾:20¾)in)

## YARN AMOUNT
Yarn A: 11(11:12:12:13:13) balls
Yarn B: 7(7:8:8:9:9) balls

## SHADES USED IN VERSION SHOWN
Yarn A: Chestnut 703
Yarn B: Natural 701

## SUGGESTED NEEDLES
3.5mm (UK 9/10, US 4) and 4mm (UK 8, US 6) long and short circular needles and dpns. Change from long to short circular needle and to dpns as number of sts and diameter of work decreases and vice versa.

> **TIP:** To ensure a good result when knitting with two or more colours, always hold yarns in the same position behind the work. Decide to keep the background colour innermost and the contrast colour outermost, for example.

## TENSION (GAUGE)
24 sts and 28 rounds to approx 10cm (4in) over stocking (stockinette) stitch using 4mm (UK 8, US 6) needles. Remember that you need to maintain an even tension for a successful result. Check your tension by knitting a test swatch. Count the number of stitches per 10cm (4in). If you have more stitches than stated, go up a needle size. If you have fewer stitches, switch to smaller needles.

> **TIP:** The tension will be tighter when working the Fair Isle pattern and it is often useful to go up 0.5mm or 1mm in needle size (one or two UK/US sizes).

## BODY

Cast on 228(246:264:282:306:306) sts using 3.5mm (UK 9/10, US 4) circular needle and yarn A. Work approx 6cm (2½in) in k1, p1 rib in the round for all sizes. Change to 4mm (UK 8, US 6) circular needle. Place marker at each side, marking 115(123:133:141:153:153) sts for front and 113(123:131:141:153:153) sts for back. Work in the round in patt following chart. Cont until work measures approx 48(49:50:51:52:53)cm (19(19¼:19¾:20:20½:20¾)in) from cast on edge. Cast (bind) off 14 sts on each side, 7 sts each side of marker. Set aside while you knit sleeves.

## SLEEVES

Cast on 54(54:58:58:60:60) sts using 3.5mm (UK 9/10, US 4) dpns and yarn A. Work 6cm (2½in) in k1, p1 rib in the round. Change to 4mm (UK 8, US 6) needles and knit 1 round increasing evenly across round to 69(71:73:77:79:79) sts. Place marker at beg of round = centre underarm. Work in the round following patt as shown in chart at the same time increasing 1 st each side of marker approx every 4(4:3.5:3.5:3.5:3.5)cm (1½(1½:1⅜:1⅜:1⅜:1⅜)in) until there are 89(93:97:101:105:105) sts in total. Work until sleeve measures stated or desired length. Make sure to end with same round of chart as for body. Cast (bind) off 14 sts at centre underarm, 7 sts each side of marker. Set aside and work other sleeve the same way.

## YOKE

Place all pieces on the same 4mm (UK 8, US 6) circular needle with one sleeve positioned over each set of cast (bound) off sts on body. 350(376:402:428:460:460) rem sts. Place markers at all four joins. Cont in same patt as before, working decreases at all four joins. Work all raglan decreases using yarn A: work until 4 sts before marker, sl1 loosely, k1, psso, p1, k2, p1, k2tog. 8 sts decreased in round. Dec in the same way on alt rounds until you have worked raglan decrease round 24(27:29:32:35:35) times in total. On next round, cast (bind) off centre 23(25:31:33:39:39) sts on front for neck. Work to end of round. Break yarn

and beg at front after cast (bound) off sts. Check that you are starting on RS and with a raglan decrease row so that you are not working raglan decreases on a WS row. Work back and forth in patt continuing raglan decreases and decreasing at each side of neck on alt rows as foll: 4, 2, 2, 1 sts. Cont until you have worked 29(32:34:37:40:40) raglan decreases on back in total. 77(77:81:81:83:83) rem sts. Work neckband.

## NECKBAND

Move rem sts to 3.5mm (UK 9/10, US 4) circular needle. Using yarn A, pick up 39(39:45:47:53:53) sts from front neck. 116(116:126:128:136:136) rem sts. Cont in k1, p1 rib in the round until neckband measures approx 3cm (1¼in). Purl 1 round (forms foldline). Work 3cm (1¼in) in rib. Cast (bind) off loosely in rib. Fold neck edge over to WS and sew down loosely.

## MAKING UP

Sew together at underarms. Weave in all loose ends on WS.

## CHART

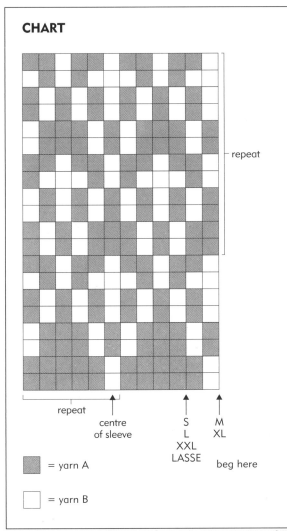

repeat

repeat

centre
of sleeve

S
L
XXL
LASSE

M
XL

beg here

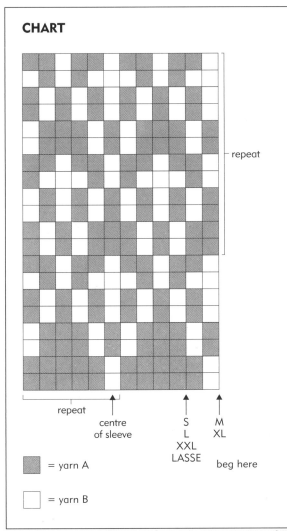= yarn A

= yarn B

# MOUNTAINTOP SWEATER
## WOMEN

**YARN**

Gann Garn Myk Merino (100% superwash merino wool, 50g (1¾oz) = approx 120m (131yd))

**DIFFICULTY**

Experienced

**SIZES**

XS(S:M:L:XL:XXL)
See garment measurements to check sizing

**GARMENT MEASUREMENTS**

Chest approx 85(93:103:109:120:130)cm
(33½(36½:40½:43:47¼:51)in)
Length approx 56(58:60:62:64:66)cm
(22(22¾:23½:24½:25¼:26)in)
Sleeve length approx 48cm (19in) or desired length

**YARN AMOUNT**

Yarn A: 9(9:10:10:11:11) balls
Yarn B: 6(6:7:7:8:8) balls

**SHADES USED IN VERSION SHOWN**

Yarn A: Chestnut 703
Yarn B: Natural 701

**SUGGESTED NEEDLES**

3.5mm (UK 9/10, US 4) and 4mm (UK 8, US 6) long and short circular needles and dpns. Change from long to short circular needle and to dpns as number of sts and diameter of work decreases and vice versa.

**TIP:** To ensure a good result when knitting with two or more colours, always hold yarns in the same position behind the work. Decide to keep the background colour innermost and the contrast colour outermost, for example.

**TENSION (GAUGE)**

24 sts and 28 rounds to approx 10cm (4in) over stocking (stockinette) stitch using 4mm (UK 8, US 6) needles. Remember that you need to maintain an even tension for a successful result. Check your tension by knitting a test swatch. Count the number of stitches per 10cm (4in). If you have more stitches than stated, go up a needle size. If you have fewer stitches, switch to smaller needles.

**BODY**

Cast on 204(222:246:264:288:312) sts using 3.5mm (UK 9/10, US 4) circular needle and yarn A. Work approx 6cm (2½in) in twisted rib (k1TBL, p1) in the round for all sizes. Change to 4mm (UK 8, US 6) circular needle. Place marker at each side, marking 103(111:123:133:145:157) sts for front and 101(111:123:131:143:155) sts for back. Work in the round in patt following chart. Cont until work measures approx 37(38:39:40:41:42)cm (14½(15:15¼:15¾:16¼:16½)in). Cast (bind) off 12 sts on each side, 6 sts each side of marker. Set work aside while you knit sleeves.

## SLEEVES

Cast on 48(48:52:52:56:56) sts using 3.5mm (UK 9/10, US 4) dpns and yarn A. Work 6cm (2½in) in k1, p1 rib in the round. Change to 4mm (UK 8, US 6) needles and knit 1 round increasing evenly across round to 57(61:65:69:73:77) sts. Place marker at beg of round = centre underarm. Count out from centre to determine start of patt and work in the round in patt following chart at the same time as increasing 1 st each side of marker approx every 3.5(3:3:3:3:3)cm (1⅜(1¼:1¼:1¼:1¼:1¼)in) until there are 81(87:91:95:101:105) sts. Work until sleeve measures stated or desired length. Make sure to end with same round of chart as for body. On last round, cast (bind) off 12 sts at centre underarm, 6 sts each side of marker. Set aside and work other sleeve the same way.

## YOKE

Place all pieces on the same 4mm (UK 8, US 6) circular needle with one sleeve positioned over each set of cast (bound) off sts on body. 318(348:380:406:442:474) rem sts. Mark 1 st at each join, placing markers in first st counting from body. 4 sts marked in round. Cont in same patt as before, working decreases at all four joins. Always decrease using yarn A: work until 2 sts before marker, sl1 loosely, k1, psso, k2, k2tog. 8 sts decreased in round. Dec in the same way on alt rounds until you have worked raglan decrease round 22(24:27:30:33:36) times in total. On next round, cast (bind) off centre 17(21:27:31:37:43) sts on front for neck. Work to end of round. Break yarn and beg at front after cast (bound) off sts. Check that you are starting raglan decreases on RS. Work back and forth in patt continuing raglan decreases, and dec at each side of neck on alt rows as foll: 4, 2, 2, 1 sts. Cont until you have worked 27(29:32:35:38:41) raglan decreases on back in total = 67(77:79:77:83:85) rem sts. Work neckband.

## NECKBAND

Move rem sts to 3.5mm (UK 9/10, US 4) circular needle and using yarn A, pick up 37(39:45:49:55:61) sts from front neck. Approx 102(114:120:124:136:144) rem sts. Cont in twisted rib (k1TBL, p1) in the round until neckband measures approx 6cm (2½in). Cast (bind) off loosely in rib. Fold neck edge over to WS and sew down loosely.

## MAKING UP

Sew together at underarms. Weave in all loose ends on WS.

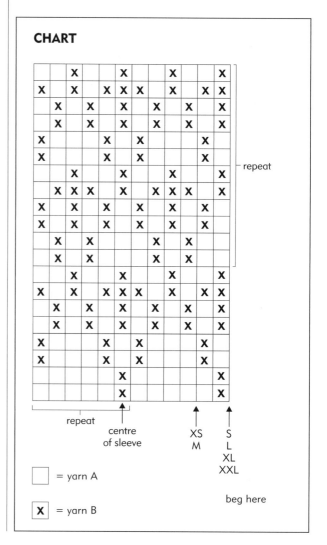

**CHART**

repeat

repeat

centre of sleeve

XS
M

S
L
XL
XXL

beg here

☐ = yarn A

☒ = yarn B

# MOUNTAINTOP SWEATER
## CHILDREN

The soft merino yarn used for this sweater means that even the youngest members of the family will love Mountaintop.

**YARN**
Gann Garn Myk Merino (100% superwash merino wool, 50g (1¾oz) = approx 120m (131yd))

**DIFFICULTY**
Experienced

**SIZES**
Age 2–4(6:8:10:12)
See garment measurements below to check sizing

**GARMENT MEASUREMENTS**
Chest approx 60(65:70:75:80)cm
(23½(25½:27½:29½:31½)in)
Length approx 40(44:49:53:56)cm
(15¾(17¼:19¼:20¾:22)in)
Sleeve length approx 27(33:36:38:40)cm
(10¾(13:14¼:15:15¾in)

**YARN AMOUNT**
Yarn A: 4(4:5:5:6) balls
Yarn B: 3(3:4:4:5) balls

**SHADES USED IN VERSIONS SHOWN**
Yarn A: Chestnut 703
Yarn B: Caramel 704
(Alternative colourway: Beige 705 and Chestnut 703, page 65)

**SUGGESTED NEEDLES**
3.5mm (UK 9/10, US 4) and 4mm (UK 8, US 6) long and short circular needles and dpns. Change from long to short circular needle and to dpns as number of sts and diameter of work decreases and vice versa.

> **TIP:** To ensure a good result when knitting with two or more colours, always hold yarns in the same position behind the work. Decide to keep the background colour innermost and the contrast colour outermost, for example.

**TENSION (GAUGE)**
24 sts and 28 rounds to approx 10cm (4in) over stocking (stockinette) stitch using 4mm (UK 8, US 6) needles. Remember that you need to maintain an even tension for a successful result. Check your tension by knitting a test swatch. Count the number of stitches per 10cm (4in). If you have more stitches than stated, go up a needle size. If you have fewer stitches, switch to smaller needles.

**BODY**
Cast on 144(156:168:180:192) sts using 3.5mm (UK 9/10, US 4) circular needle and yarn A. Work twisted rib (k1TBL, p1) for approx 3(3:4:4:4)cm (1¼(1¼:1½:1½:1½)in).

Change to 4mm (UK 8, US 6) circular needle. Place marker at each side, marking 73(79:85:91:97) sts for front and 71(77:83:89:95) sts for back. Work in the round in patt following chart. Cont until work measures approx 27(30:34:37:39)cm (10¾(11¾:13½:14½:15¼)in). Cast (bind) off 10 sts on each side, 5 sts each side of marker. Set work aside while you knit sleeves.

### SLEEVES
Cast on 32(36:40:44:46) sts using 3.5mm (UK 9/10, US 4) dpns and yarn A. Work 3(3:4:4:4)cm (1¼(1¼:1½:1½:1½)in) in twisted rib (k1TBL, p1) in the round. Change to 4mm (UK 8, US 6) needles and knit 1 round increasing evenly across round to 53(57:61:67:73) sts. Place marker at beg of round = centre underarm. Count out from centre to determine start of patt and work in the round in patt following chart. Work until sleeve measures stated or desired length. Make sure to end with same round of chart as for body. On last round, cast (bind) off 10 sts at centre underarm, 5 sts each side of marker. Set aside and work other sleeve the same way.

### YOKE
Place all pieces on the same 4mm (UK 8, US 6) circular needle with one sleeve positioned over each set of cast (bound) off sts on body. 210(230:250:274:298) sts. Mark one stitch at each join, placing markers in first st counting from body. 4 sts marked in round. Cont in same patt as before, working decreases at all four joins. Always decrease using yarn A. Work until 2 sts before marked st, sl1 loosely, k1, psso, k2, k2tog. 8 sts decreased in round. Dec in the same way on every alt round until you have worked raglan decrease round 13(15:17:20:22) times in total. On next round cast (bind) off centre 15(17:19:19:21) sts on front for neck. Work to end of round. Break yarn and beg at front after cast (bound) off sts. Check that you are starting raglan decreases on RS. Work back and forth in patt continuing raglan decreases and decreasing at each side of neck on alt rows as foll: 3, 2 sts for all sizes. Cont until you have worked 17(19:21:24:26) raglan decreases on back in total = 49(51:53:53:59) rem sts. Work neckband.

### NECKBAND
Move rem sts to 3.5mm (UK 9/10, US 4) circular needle. Using yarn A, pick up 29(31:31:35:35) sts from front neck. Approx 78(80:82:86:92) rem sts. Cont in twisted rib (k1TBL, p1) in the round until neckband measures approx 5(5:6:6:)cm (2½(:2½:3:3:3)in). Cast (bind) off loosely in rib. Fold neck edge over to WS and sew down loosely.

### MAKING UP
Sew together at underarms. Weave in all loose ends on WS.

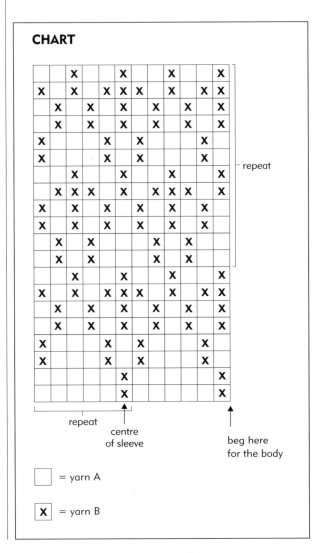

CHART

repeat

repeat

centre
of sleeve

beg here
for the body

□ = yarn A

X = yarn B

# SAILOR SWEATER

A warm but airy rib sweater great for any globetrotter. There is also a co-ordinating hat – see page 172 in the Cosy Accessories section for its instructions.

**YARN**
Gann Garn Myk Merino (100% superwash merino wool, 50g (1¾oz) = approx 120m (131yd))

**DIFFICULTY**
Experienced

**SIZES**
S(M:L:XL:XXL:LASSE)
See garment measurements below to check sizing

**GARMENT MEASUREMENTS**
Chest approx 99(108:118:127:136:127)cm (39(42½:46½:50:53½50)in)
Length approx 66(68:70:72:74:78)cm (26(26¾:27½:28¼:29¼:30¾)in)
Sleeve length approx 50(50:52:52:53:53)cm (19¾(19¾:20½:20½:20¾:20¾)in)

**YARN AMOUNT**
Yarn A: 18(19:21:23:24:25) balls
Yarn B: one ball for all sizes

**SHADES USED IN VERSION SHOWN**
Yarn A: Slate 707
Yarn B: Light grey 706

**SUGGESTED NEEDLES**
3.5mm (UK 9/10, US 4) and 4mm (UK 8, US 6) long and short circular needles and dpns

**NOTIONS**
Two 22–25mm (¾–1in) diameter buttons

**TENSION (GAUGE)**
26 sts and 32 rounds to approx 10cm (4in) over rib using 4mm (UK 8, US 6) needles.
24 sts and 28 rounds to approx 10cm (4in) over stocking (stockinette) stitch using 4mm (UK 8, US 6) needles.
Remember that you need to maintain an even tension for a successful result. Check your tension by knitting a test swatch. Count the number of stitches per 10cm (4in). If you have more stitches than stated, go up a needle size. If you have fewer stitches, switch to smaller needles.

## BODY

Cast on 218(238:258:280:300:280) sts using 3.5mm (UK 9/10, US 4) circular needle and yarn A.
Work 4cm (1½in) in stocking (stockinette) stitch in the round. Purl 1 round (forms foldline). Work 4cm (1½in) in stocking (stockinette) stitch. At the same time, on last round inc 38(42:46:48:52:48) sts evenly across round to 256(280:304:328:352:328) sts. There are now 128(140:152:164:176:164) sts each for front and back. Place marker in first and last st on front = side markers.
Change to 4mm (UK 8, US 6) circular needle.
Cont in patt following chart.
When work measures 46(47:48:49:50:53)cm (18(18½:19:19¼:19¾:20¾)in) from foldline, cast (bind) off 11 sts at each side for armhole, marked sts + 5 sts either side.
Set aside while you work sleeves.

## SLEEVES

Cast on 52(52:56:56:60:60) sts using 3.5mm (UK 9/10, US 4) dpns and yarn A.
Work cuff in k3, p1 rib in the round following stripe patt. At the same time, on last round inc 11(13:13:17:15:17) sts evenly across round to 63(65:69:73:75:77) sts. Change to yarn A and 4mm (UK 8, US 6) needles. Place marker at beg of round = centre underarm. Cont in patt following chart.
At the same time, on second round, inc 1 st each side

of marker. Rep increase every 3.5(3:3:3:2.5:2.5)cm (1⅜(1¼:1¼:1¼:1:1)in) until you have worked increase round 13(14:15:17:18:18) times in total and there are 89(93:99:105:109:113) sts.
When sleeve measures 50(50:52:52:53:53)cm (19¾(19¾:20½:20½:20¾:20¾)in) or desired length, cast (bind) off 12 sts at centre underarm for armhole, 6 sts each side of marker. 77(81:87:93:97:101) rem sts. Set work aside and work other sleeve the same way.

## YOKE

Read whole section before knitting yoke.
Place all pieces on the same 4mm (UK 8, US 6) circular needle with one sleeve positioned over each set of cast (bound) off sts on body. 388(420:456:492:524:508) sts. Place marker at each join. 4 markers in round. Cont in patt as before, using yarn A. At the same time, in round 1 of yoke work raglan decrease at all markers: work until 2 sts before marker, sl1 loosely, k1, psso, k2tog. 8 sts decreased in round. Work raglan decreases on every round until there are 5(6:7:8:9:10) decrease rounds. Now cont decreasing sleeve sts only on alt rounds while working body sts straight up with no decreasing. 4 sts decreased in round. Work these decrease rounds 26(27:28:30:30:31) times. 15(15:17:17:19:19) shoulder sts rem on each sleeve. At the same time, once you have worked 5(6:7:8:9:10)cm (2(2½:2¾:3¼:3½:4)in) from beg of yoke, cast (bind) off centre 6 sts on front for neck.
Work back and forth in patt continuing to decrease for raglan at sleeves. At the same time, once you have worked another 5cm (2in), dec 2 sts on each side for neck on alt rows 12(12:12:13:13:12) times in total. Once you have completed the sleeve decreases, decrease for shoulder: work front until 1 st rem (you are now at shoulder stitches), sl1, k1 from shoulder, psso, work 13(13:15:15:17:17) shoulder sts in patt as before, k2tog, work back until 1 st rem and rep decrease as for right shoulder. 4 sts decreased in row. Rep this decrease on each row.

On WS p2tog to decrease. When the neck decreases reach shoulder decreases, only decrease at tops of shoulders on back.

Once you have decreased 26(30:35:39:44:38) times at each side of back and all neck sts have been decreased as shown, place 56(58:58:60:60:58) sts from back, and 15(15:17:17:19:19) sts from each shoulder and 0(1:1:0:0:1) sts from each side of the front on a holder. 86(90:94:94:98:98) rem sts.

## NECKBAND

Beg from RS at right neck edge. Using yarn A and a 4mm (UK 8, US 6) circular needle, work or pick up approx 11 sts per 5cm (2in) along right neck edge, work neck sts and pick up along left neck edge in same way. Number of sts must be divisible by 4 – 1 st. Place markers for 2 buttonholes on left side, the first 1cm (⅜in) from beg of neck edge and the other approx 4cm (1½in) from beg of neck edge. Work 3cm (1¼in) back and forth in rib (p3, k1 on WS, k3, p1 on RS). At the same time, after 1.5cm (½in) work a buttonhole at each marker by working k2tog, yo, yo, k2togTBL. On next round work p1, k1 using yarn overs. Cast (bind) off.

Overlap ends of neckband and sew to front.

## MAKING UP

Graft or sew together at underarms.

Fold bottom edge of body to WS and sew down loosely. Sew on buttons.

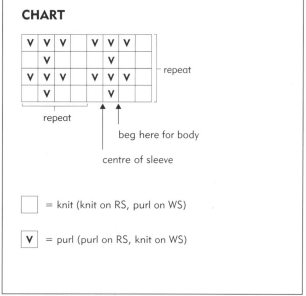

**CHART**

repeat

beg here for body

centre of sleeve

repeat

☐ = knit (knit on RS, purl on WS)

V = purl (purl on RS, knit on WS)

# SAILOR SWEATER
## CHILDREN

This sweater is super for adventurers large and small.
The pattern for the co-ordinating hat is on page 174.

**YARN**
Gann Garn Myk Merino (100% superwash
merino wool, 50g (1¾oz) = approx 120m (131yd))

**DIFFICULTY**
Experienced

**SIZES**
Age 2(4:6:8:10:12)
See garment measurements below to check sizing

**GARMENT MEASUREMENTS**
Chest approx 61(64:70:74:80:86)cm
(24(25¼:27½:29¼:31½:33¾)in)
Length approx 36(40:44:48:52:56)cm
(14¼(15¾:17¼:19:20½:22)in)
Sleeve length approx 24(27:33:36:38:40)cm
(9½(10¾:13:14¼:15:15¾)in)

**YARN AMOUNT**
Yarn A: 6(7:8:9:11:12) balls
Yarn B: one ball for all sizes

**SHADES USED IN VERSIONS SHOWN**
Yarn A: Blue 714
Yarn B: Caramel 704
(Alternative colourway: Heather 721 and Beige 705,
page 73)

**SUGGESTED NEEDLES**
4mm (UK 8, US 6) and 4.5mm (UK 7, US 7) circular
needles and dpns

**TENSION (GAUGE)**
25 sts and 32 rounds to approx 10cm (4in) over
pattern using 4.5mm (UK 7, US 7) needles.
Remember that you need to maintain an even tension
for a successful result. Check your tension by knitting
a test swatch. Count the number of stitches per 10cm
(4in). If you have more stitches than stated, go up
a needle size. If you have fewer stitches, switch to
smaller needles.

## BODY

Cast on 152(160:176:184:200:216) sts using 4.5mm (UK 7, US 7) circular needle and yarn A. Cont in the round in patt following chart. Place marker at each side, marking 77(81:89:93:101:109) sts for front and 75(79:87:91:99:107) sts for back.

When work measures 22(25:28:31:34:37)cm (8¾(9¾:11:12¼:13½:14½)in) from cast on edge, divide and work front and back separately.

## BACK

Work back and forth in patt as before apart from 1 edge st at each side which is always knit.

When work measures 12(13:14:15:16:17)cm, (4¾(5:5½:6:6¼:6¾)in) from divide, cast (bind) off centre 37(37:39:39:41:41) sts for neck. Work each side separately.

Work back and forth in patt. At the same time, cast (bind) off 1st at neck on every alt row until there are 17(19:22:24:27:31) shoulder sts. Cont until work measures approx 36(40:44:48:52:56)cm (14¼(15¾:17¼19:20½:22)in). Place sts on a holder. Work the other side the same way, reversing the neck shaping.

## FRONT

Work as for back until work measures 10(11:12:12:13:14)cm (4(4¼:4¾:4¾:5:5½)in). Cast (bind) off centre 19(19:21:21:23:23) sts for neck. Work each side separately.

Work back and forth in patt as set. At the same time, dec for neck on alt rows as foll: 4, 3, 2, 2, 1 sts. 17(19:22:24:27:31) rem shoulder sts. Cont until work measures approx 36(40:44:48:52:56)cm (14¼(15¾:17¼19:20½:22)in). Place sts on a holder. Work the other side the same way, reversing the neck shaping.

## SLEEVES

Cast on 32(32:36:36:40:40) sts using 4mm (UK 8, US 6) dpns and yarn A. Work 4(4:4:5:5:5)cm (1½:1½:1½:2:2:2)in) in k1, p1 rib in the round. At the same time, on last row inc 19(19:17:19:17:21) sts evenly across round to 51(51:53:55:57:61) sts. Change to 4.5mm (UK 7, US 7) needles.

Place marker at beg of round = centre underarm. Cont in patt following chart. Count out from centre sleeve to determine start of pattern. At the same time, on second round, inc 1 st each side of marker. Rep increases approx every 2cm (¾in) in all sizes until you have worked increase round 10(12:14:15:16:17) times in total. 71(75:81:85:85:89:95) rem sts. Work increased sts into pattern.

When sleeve measures 24(27:33:36:38:40)cm (9½(10¾:13:14¼:15:15¾)in) or desired length, cast (bind) off all sts loosely in patt.
Knit other sleeve the same way.

## MAKING UP

Graft or sew together at shoulders.

## NECKBAND

Place marker at centre front of neck. Beg at back of neck at right shoulder seam. Using 4mm (UK 8, US 6) circular needle and yarn A, pick up 82(86:90:94:98:102) sts around whole neck. Number of sts must be divisible by 2 and the same on both sides of the marker.

Work 4 rounds in k1, p1 rib.

Place marker approx 3cm (1¼in) from each side of centre marker. Make a hole at each marker by working k2tog, yo. Work 12 more rounds in rib in all sizes.

Cast (bind) off loosely in rib.

Fold neck edge over to WS and sew down loosely on the seam between neck and yoke.

## CORD
Cast on 4 sts using 4mm (UK 8, US 6) dpns and yarn B and work in the round: *slide sts to right of needle, tighten yarn at back, k4*. Rep from * to * until cord measures approx 75(75:80:80:85:85)cm (29½(29½:31½:31½:33½:33½) or desired length. Cast (bind) off. Alternatively, use an i-cord maker or French knitting machine.

## MAKING UP
Graft or sew in sleeves. Thread cord through casing in neckband.

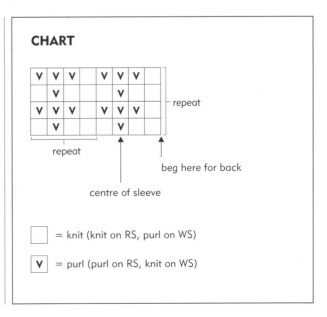

**CHART**

repeat

beg here for back

centre of sleeve

repeat

☐ = knit (knit on RS, purl on WS)

**V** = purl (purl on RS, knit on WS)

# BREEZE SWEATER

Soft, roomy and as warm as the Lasse sweater, the Breeze sweater comes in a range of sizes for the whole family. The pattern for the matching hat is on page 170.

## YARN
Gann Garn Sky (62% baby alpaca, 16% acrylic, 22% nylon, 50g (1¾oz) = approx 150m (164yd))

## DIFFICULTY
Experienced

## SIZES
S(M:L:XL:XXL:LASSE)
See garment measurements to check sizing.

## GARMENT MEASUREMENTS
Chest approx 97(109:114:125:137:125)cm
(38¼(43:44¾:49¼:54:53½)in)
Length approx 66(68:70:72:74:76)cm
(26(26¾:27½:28¼:29¼:30)in)
Sleeve length approx 50(50:52:52:53:53)cm
(19¾(19¾:20½:20½:20¾:20¾)in)

## YARN AMOUNT
Yarn A: 6(7:7:8:9:8) balls
Yarn B: 5(5:6:6:7:6) balls

## SHADES USED IN VERSION SHOWN
Yarn A: Grey melange 607
Yarn B: Natural 601

## SUGGESTED NEEDLES
5mm (UK 6, US 8) and 6mm (UK 4, US 10) long and short circular needles and dpns. Change from long to short circular needle and to dpns as number of sts and diameter of work decreases and vice versa.

> **TIP:** To ensure a good result when knitting with two or more colours, always hold yarns in the same position behind the work. Decide to keep the background colour innermost and the contrast colour outermost, for example.

## TENSION (GAUGE)
19 sts and 19 rounds to approx 10cm (4in) over pattern using 6mm (UK 4, US 10) needles.
Remember that you need to maintain an even tension for a successful result. Check your tension by knitting a test swatch. Count the number of stitches per 10cm (4in). If you have more stitches than stated, go up a needle size. If you have fewer stitches, switch to smaller needles.
Most people knit more tightly with several colours than they do when knitting ordinary stocking (stockinette) stitch. This means it's a good idea to pay extra attention to your tension and possibly go up 0.5mm or 1mm in needle size (1 or 2 UK/US sizes).

## BODY

Cast on 180(204:216:240:264:240) sts using 5mm (UK 6, US 8) circular needle and yarn A. Work 1 round in k2, p2 rib. Cont in rib in stripes: *2 rounds using yarn B, 2 rounds using yarn A*. Rep from * to *. Work until rib measures approx 6cm (2½in) for all sizes. Change to 6mm (UK 4, US 10) circular needle. Place marker at each side, marking 90(102:108:120:132:120) sts each for front and back. Beg at arrow for chosen size and cont working in the round following patt as shown in chart.
Cont until work measures approx 47(47:48:50:47:50)cm (18½(18½:19:19¾:18½:19¾)in). Cast (bind) off 12 sts on each side for armhole, 6 sts each side of marker. Set work aside while you knit sleeves.

## SLEEVES

Cast on 40(44:44:48:48:48) sts using 5mm (UK 6, US 8) dpns and yarn A. Work 6cm (2½in) in striped rib in the round as for bottom of body. Change to 6mm (UK 4, US 10) needles and work 1 round increasing evenly across round to 52(56:56:60:64:60) sts. Place marker at beg of round = centre underarm. Count out from centre to determine start of pattern. Work in the round in patt following chart at the same time increasing 1 st each side of marker approx every 3.5(3.5:3:3:3:3)cm (1⅜(1⅜:1¼:1¼:1¼:1¼)in) until there are 76(80:84:88:92:88) sts. Work until sleeve measures stated or desired length. Make sure to end with same round of chart as for body. Cast (bind) off 12 sts at centre underarm, 6 sts each side of marker. Set aside and work other sleeve the same way.

## YOKE

Place all pieces on the same 6mm (UK 4, US 10) circular needle with one sleeve positioned over each set of cast (bound) off sts on body. 284(316:336:368:400:368) sts. Mark 1 st at each join, placing markers in first st counting from body. Work in the round in patt as set, decreasing at all four joins. Always decrease using yarn A:

work until 2 sts before marked st, sl1 loosely, k1, psso, k1 (marked st), k2tog. 8 sts decreased in round. Dec on every round until you have worked raglan decrease round 10(11:13:15:18:15) times in total. Then decrease on alt rounds until you have worked raglan decrease round 19(21:23:27:31:27) times in total. On next round, cast (bind) off centre 18(26:28:32:36:32) sts on front for neck. Work to end of round. Break yarn and beg at front after cast (bound) off sts. Check that you are starting raglan decreases on RS. Work back and forth in patt, continuing to decrease for raglan and decreasing for neck at each side of neck edge on alt rows as foll: 3, 2, 1 sts in all sizes. Cont until you have worked 23(25:27:31:35:31) raglan decreases on back in total. 70(78:80:76:72:76) rem sts. Work neckband.

## NECKBAND

Move rem sts to 5mm (UK 6, US 8) circular needle and using yarn A, pick up sts from centre neck to approx 100(114:120:120:120:120) sts. Knit one round decreasing evenly to 92(96:100:100:100:100) sts. Cont in k2, p2 rib and stripes as for bottom of body and sleeve cuffs. Cont until neckband measures approx 8cm (3¼in). Cast (bind) off loosely in rib. Fold neck edge over to WS and sew down loosely.

## MAKING UP

Sew together at underarms. Weave in all loose ends on WS.

## CHART

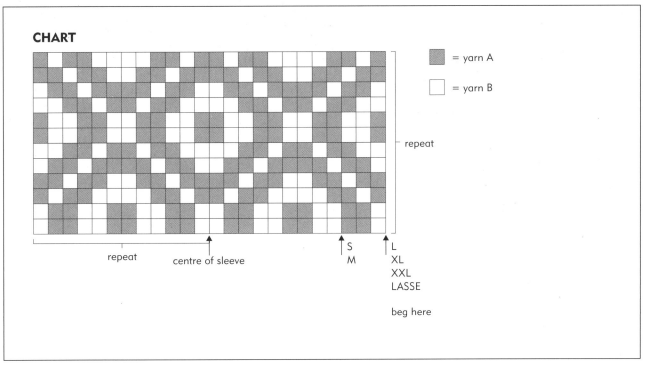

= yarn A

= yarn B

repeat

repeat   centre of sleeve

S
M

L
XL
XXL
LASSE

beg here

# BREEZE SWEATER
## WOMEN

**YARN**
Gann Garn Sky (62% baby alpaca, 16% acrylic, 22% nylon, 50g (1¾oz) = approx 150m (164yd))

**DIFFICULTY**
Experienced

**SIZES**
XS(S:M:L:XL:XXL)
See garment measurements to check sizing

**GARMENT MEASUREMENTS**
Chest approx 93(99:105:116:122:133)cm
(36½(39:41½:45½:48:52¼)in)
Length approx 56(58:60:62:64:66)cm
(22(22¾:23½:24½:25¼:26)in)
Sleeve length approx 48cm (19in) or desired length

**YARN AMOUNT**
Yarn A: 6(6:7:7:8:9) balls
Yarn B: 3(3:3:4:4:4) balls

**SHADES USED IN VERSIONS SHOWN**
Yarn A: Cognac 604
Yarn B: Natural 601
(Alternative colourway: Natural 601 and Grey melange 607, page 81)

**SUGGESTED NEEDLES**
5mm (UK 6, US 8) and 6mm (UK 4, US 10) long and short circular needles and dpns. Change from long to short circular needle and to dpns as number of sts and diameter of work decreases and vice versa.

> **TIP:** To ensure a good result when knitting with two or more colours, always hold yarns in the same position behind the work. Decide to keep the background colour innermost and the contrast colour outermost, for example.

**TENSION (GAUGE)**
19 sts and 19–20 rounds to approx 10cm (4in) over pattern using 6mm (UK 4, US 10) needles.
19 sts and 22 rounds to approx 10cm (4in) over stocking (stockinette) stitch using 6mm (UK 4, US 10) needles. Remember that you need to maintain an even tension for a successful result. Check your tension by knitting a test swatch. Count the number of stitches per 10cm (4in). If you have more stitches than stated, go up a needle size. If you have fewer stitches, switch to smaller needles.

## BODY

Cast on 176(188:196:220:232:252) sts using 5mm (UK 6, US 8) circular needle and yarn A. Work 1 round in k2, p2 rib. Cont in rib in stripes: *2 rounds using yarn B, 2 rounds using yarn A.* Rep from * to *. Work until rib measures approx 6cm (2½in) or until you have worked 3 stripes using yarn B in all sizes. End with 2 rounds using yarn A. Change to 6mm (UK 4, US 10) circular needle. Place marker at each side, marking 88(94:98:110:116:126) sts each for front and back. Work in stocking (stockinette) stitch using yarn A until work measures approx 36(37:38:39:40:41)cm (14¼(14½:15:15¼:15¾:16¼) in). Cast (bind) off 10 sts on each side, 5 sts each side of marker at underarms. Set work aside while you knit sleeves.

## SLEEVES

Cast on 36(36:40:40:44:44) sts using 5mm (UK 6, US 8) dpns and yarn A. Work 6cm (2½in) in striped rib in the round as for bottom of body. Change to 6mm (UK 4, US 10) needles. Knit 1 round using yarn A, increasing evenly across round to 42(44:46:50:52:54) sts. Place marker at beg of round = centre underarm. Work in the round in stocking (stockinette) stitch using yarn A while increasing 1 st on each side of marker approx every 3.5(3:3:3:2.5:2.5)cm (1⅜(1¼:1¼:1¼:1:1)in) to a total 68(72:76:80:82:86) sts. Work until sleeve measures stated or desired length. Cast (bind) off 10 sts at centre underarm, 5 sts each side of marker. Set aside and work other sleeve the same way.

## YOKE

Place all pieces on the same 6mm (UK 4, US 10) circular needle with one sleeve positioned over each set of cast (bound) off sts on body. 272(292:308:340:356:384) sts. Work in the round in patt following chart. Count from centre front to determine where pattern should begin for each section: back, left sleeve, front, right sleeve. At the same time mark 1 st at each join, placing markers 1 st in from body.

4 sts marked in round. Always decrease using yarn A: work until 2 sts before marked st, k2togTBL, k1 (marked st), k2tog. Work decreases at all four joins. 8 sts decreased in round. Dec on every round 5(7:9:11:13:15) times and then every alt round until you have worked raglan decrease round 19(21:23:26:28:31) times in total. On next round, cast (bind) off centre 18(20:20:26:28:32) sts on front for neck. Work to end of round. Break yarn and beg from front after cast (bound) off sts. Check that you are starting raglan decreases on RS. Work back and forth in patt, continuing to decrease for raglan and decreasing for neck at each side of neck edge on every alt row as follows: 3, 2, 1 sts in all sizes. Work until you have worked 23(25:27:30:32:35) raglan decreases on back in total. 58(60:60:62:60:60) rem sts. Work neckband.

## NECKBAND

Move rem sts to 5mm (UK 6, US 8) circular needle and using yarn A, pick up 30(32:32:34:40:40) sts from front neck. 88(92:92:96:100:100) sts. Cont in k2, p2 rib and stripes as for bottom of body and sleeve cuffs. Alternate stripes in this way until neckband measures approx 16cm (6¼in). Cast (bind) off loosely in rib.

## MAKING UP

Sew together at underarms. Weave in all loose ends on WS.

## CHART

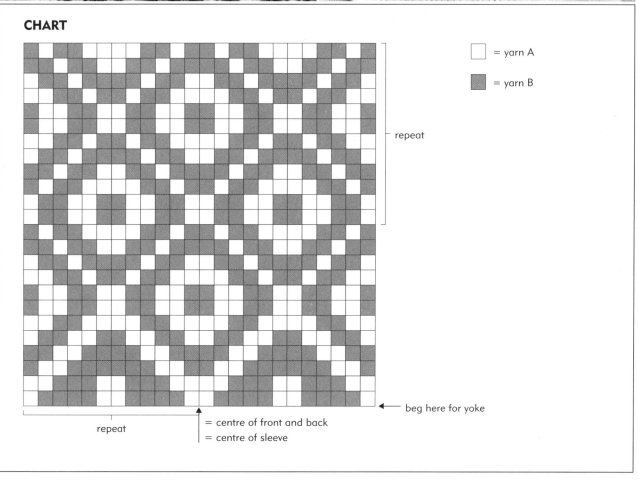

□ = yarn A

■ = yarn B

repeat

← beg here for yoke

repeat

= centre of front and back
= centre of sleeve

# BREEZE SWEATER
## CHILDREN

**YARN**
Gann Garn Sky (62% baby alpaca, 16% acrylic,
22% nylon, 50g (1¾oz) = approx 150m (164yd))

**DIFFICULTY**
Experienced

**SIZES**
Age 2–4(6:8:10:12)
See garment measurements to check sizing.

**GARMENT MEASUREMENTS**
Chest approx 63(69:76:82:88)cm
(24¾(27¼:29¼:31½:33¾)in)
Length approx 38(44:48:52:56)cm
(15(17¼:19:20½:22)in)
Sleeve length approx 26(33:36:38:40)cm
(10¼(13:14¼:15:15¾)in)

**YARN AMOUNT**
Yarn A: 2(3:3:3:4) balls
Yarn B: 2(2:2:3:3) balls

**SHADES USED IN VERSIONS SHOWN**
Yarn A: Navy 615
Yarn B: Natural 601
(Alternative colourway: Wine 608 and Natural 601,
page 85)

**SUGGESTED NEEDLES**
5mm (UK 6, US 8) and 6mm (UK 4, US 10) long and
short circular needles and dpns. Change from long
to short circular needle and to dpns as number of sts
and diameter of work decreases and vice versa.

> **TIP:** To ensure a good result when knitting with
> two or more colours, always hold yarns in the
> same position behind the work. Decide to keep
> the background colour innermost and the contrast
> colour outermost, for example.

**TENSION (GAUGE)**
19 sts and 19–20 rounds to approx 10cm (4in) over
pattern using 6mm (UK 4, US 10) needles.
Remember that you need to maintain an even tension
for a successful result. Check your tension by knitting
a test swatch. Count the number of stitches per 10cm
(4in). If you have more stitches than stated, go up
a needle size. If you have fewer stitches, switch to
smaller needles.

## BODY

Cast on 120(132:144:156:168) sts using 5mm (UK 6, US 8) circular needle and yarn A. Work 1 round in k2, p2 rib. Cont in rib in stripes: *1 round using yarn B, 2 rounds using yarn A.* Rep from * to *. Work until rib measures approx 4(4:5:5:6)cm (1½(1½:2:2:2½)in). Change to 6mm (UK 4, US 10) needle. Place marker at each side, marking 60(66:72:78:84) sts each for front and back. Work in stocking (stockinette) stitch in patt in the round until work measures approx 23(28:31:35:38)cm (9(11:12¼: 13¾:15)in). Cast (bind) off 10 sts on each side, 5 sts each side of marker. Set aside while you knit sleeves.

## SLEEVES

Cast on 24(28:28:32:32) sts using 5mm (UK 6, US 8) dpns and yarn A. Work 6cm (2½in) in the round in striped rib as for bottom of body. Change to 6mm (UK 4, US 10) needles. Knit 1 round using yarn A, at the same time increasing evenly across round to 36(38:40:42:44) sts. Place marker at beg of round = centre underarm. Count out from centre sleeve to determine start of patt. Work in the round in stocking (stockinette) stitch in patt as shown in chart, at the same time increasing 1 st each side of marker approx every 3(4.5:3.5:4:4)cm (1¼(1¾:1⅜:1½:1½)in) until there are 50(50:56:58:60) sts in total. Work until sleeve measures stated or desired length. Make sure to end with same round of chart as for body. On last round, cast (bind) off 10 sts at centre underarm, 5 sts each side of marker. Set aside and work other sleeve the same way.

## YOKE

Place all pieces on the same 6mm (UK 4, US 10) circular needle with one sleeve positioned over each set of cast (bound) off sts on body = 180(192:216:232:248) sts. Work in the round in patt following chart. At the same time mark 1 st at each join, placing markers in first st counting from body. This st is always worked using yarn A.
Dec for raglan using yarn A: work until 2 sts before marked st, sl1 loosely, k1, psso, k1 (marked st), k2tog. Work decreases at all four joins. 8 sts decreased in round. Dec in the same way on every alt round until you have worked raglan decrease round 10(11:13:15:17) times in total. Cont decreasing for neck. Cast (bind) off centre 10(14:16:18:20) sts on front. Work to end of round. Break yarn and beg at front after cast (bound) off sts. Check that you are starting raglan decreases on RS. Work back and forth in patt, continuing to decrease for raglan and decreasing for neck at each side of neck edge on alt rows as foll: 2, 2, 1 sts. Cont until you have worked 14(15:17:19:21) raglan decreases on back in total. 48(48:54:52:50) rem sts. Work neckband.

## NECKBAND

Move rem sts to 5mm (UK 6, US 8) circular needle and using yarn A, pick up approx 20(24:26:28:34) sts from front neck to approx 68(72:80:80:84) sts. Cont in k2, p2 rib and stripes as for bottom of body and sleeve cuffs. Work alternate stripes until neckband measures approx 6(6:7:7:7)cm (2½(2½:2¾:2¾:2¾)in). Cast (bind) off loosely in rib. Fold neck edge over to WS and sew down loosely.

## MAKING UP

Sew together at underarms. Weave in all loose ends on WS.

## CHART

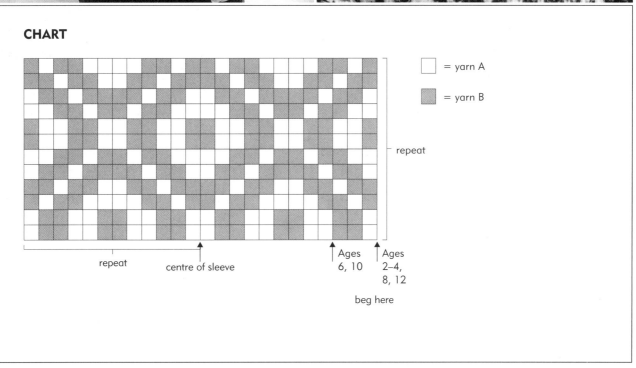

= yarn A

= yarn B

repeat

repeat        centre of sleeve        ↑ Ages 6, 10     ↑ Ages 2–4, 8, 12

beg here

# SAGA SWEATER

The Saga sweater is a favourite. Inspired by the Icelandic sweater, it's guaranteed to withstand harsh weather. The men's version is designed to fit especially well across the shoulders.

**YARN**
Gann Garn Myk Merino (100% superwash merino wool, 50g (1¾oz) = approx 120m (131yd))

**DIFFICULTY**
Experienced

**SIZES**
S(M:L:XL:XXL:LASSE)
See garment measurements to check sizing

**GARMENT MEASUREMENTS**
Chest approx 98(109:115:125:136:131)cm
(38½(43:45¼:49¼:53½:51¼)in)
Length approx 66(68:70:72:74:78)cm
(26(26¾:27½:28¼:29¼:30¾)in)
Sleeve length approx 50(50:52:52:53:53)cm
(19¾(19¾:20½:20½:20¾:20¾)in)

**YARN AMOUNT**
Yarn A: 10(11:12:13:14:14) balls
Yarn B: 4(5:5:6:6:6) balls

**SHADES USED IN VERSION SHOWN**
Yarn A: Slate 707
Yarn B: Natural 701

**SUGGESTED NEEDLES**
4mm (UK 8, US 6) and 4.5mm (UK 7, US 7) long and short circular needles and dpns. Change from long to short circular needle and to dpns as number of sts and diameter of work decreases and vice versa.

> **TIP:** The tension will be tighter when working the Fair Isle pattern and it is often useful to go up 0.5mm or 1mm in needle size (one or two UK/US sizes).

**TENSION (GAUGE)**
22 sts and 28 rounds to approx 10cm (4in) over stocking (stockinette) stitch using 4.5mm (UK 7, US 7) needles. Remember that you need to maintain an even tension for a successful result. Check your tension by knitting a test swatch. Count the number of stitches per 10cm (4in). If you have more stitches than stated, go up a needle size. If you have fewer stitches, switch to smaller needles.

## BODY

Cast on 216(240:252:276:300:288) sts using 4mm (UK 8, US 6) circular needle and yarn A. Work k2, p2 rib in stripe patt: *work 3 rounds using yarn A, 3 rounds using yarn B* (cast on counts as round 1). Rep from * to * twice. Change to 4.5mm (UK 7, US 7) circular needle. Place marker at each side, marking 108(120:126:138:150) sts each for front and back. Cont in patt following chart. When work measures 46(47:48:49:50:53)cm (18(18½:19:19¼:19¾:20¾)in) from cast on edge, cast (bind) off 12 sts at each side for armhole, 6 sts either side of markers. Set aside while you work sleeves.

## SLEEVES

Cast on 50(52:54:56:60:60) sts using 4mm (UK 8, US 6) dpns and yarn A. Work rib and stripe patt in the round as for body. At the same time, on last round inc 12(14:16:18:18:16) sts evenly to 62(66:70:74:78:76) sts.
Change to 4.5mm (UK 7, US 7) needles. Place marker at beg of round = centre underarm.
Work patt following chart and count out from centre sleeve to determine start of patt.
At the same time, on round 2, inc 1 st each side of marker. Rep increase every 3(3:3.5:3:3:2.5)cm (1¼(1¼:1⅜:1¼:1¼:1)in) until you have worked increase round 13(13:13:14:15:18) times in total and there are 88(92:96:102:108:112) sts.
When sleeve measures 50(50:52:52:53:53)cm (19¾(19¾:20½:20½:20¾:20¾)in) or desired length, cast (bind) off 12 sts at centre underarm for armhole, 6 sts each side of marker. Make sure last round of sleeve is the same chart row as last round of body. Set aside and work other sleeve in the same way.

## YOKE

Place all pieces on the same 4.5mm (UK 7, US 7) circular needle with one sleeve positioned over each set of cast (bound) off sts on body. 344(376:396:432:468:464) sts. Place marker at each join. 4 markers in round. Cont in patt on each section as before. At the same time, in round 1 of yoke work raglan decrease at all markers: work until 2 sts before marker, sl1 loosely, k1, psso, k2, k2tog. 8 sts decreased in round. Work raglan decreases on every round until you have worked 5(6:7:8:9:10) decrease rounds. Now cont decreasing only sleeve sts while working body sts straight up with no decrease: work decreases on sleeves every round 11(12:11:11:15:16) times, every alt round 15(15:17:18:16:16) times, 26(27:28:29:31:32) times in total. 200(220:228:252:272:256) rem sts. You now have 14(14:14:16:16:16) rem sts for each shoulder. Cont decreasing as follows, now only decreasing on front and back sts (not sleeve sts): work front until 1 st rem (you are now at shoulder st), sl1 (shoulder st), k1 from shoulder, psso. Work 12(12:12:14:14:14) sts in patt as before, k2tog. Work decreases in same way on each shoulder/front and shoulder/back on each round. 4 sts decreased in round. After working 15(20:21:26:30:26) rounds of decreases, cast (bind) off centre 26(26:28:28:30:30) sts on front for neck. Cont back and forth in stocking (stockinette) stitch and decreasing at shoulders as before, at the same time dec 1 st at each side of neck edge on every row a total six times as foll: 3, 2, 1, 1, 1, 1 sts, making a total 21(26:27:32:36:32) decreases at each shoulder. 72(72:74:78:80:80) rem sts.

## NECKBAND

Beg at back at right shoulder using 4mm (UK 8, US 6) circular needle and yarn A. Work sts at neck and left shoulder, work or pick up approx 11 sts per 5cm (2in) along front neck edge and work sts on right shoulder. Number of sts must be divisible by 4.
Work rib and stripe patt in the round as for body and sleeves until neckband measures approx 6cm (2½in). Cast (bind) off loosely in rib.
Fold neck edge over to WS and sew down loosely.

## MAKING UP

Graft or sew together at underarms.

## CHART

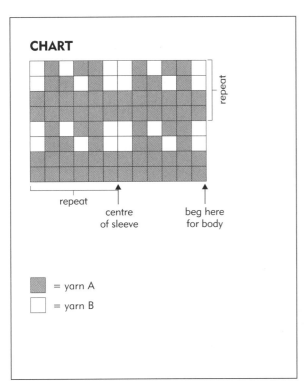

repeat

centre of sleeve

beg here for body

= yarn A

= yarn B

# SAGA SWEATER
## WOMEN

The women's version has a cosy polo neck. You can vary the ribbing on all the Saga sweaters, choosing wide or narrow stripes.

**YARN**
Gann Garn Sky (62% baby alpaca, 16% acrylic, 22% nylon, 50g (1¾oz) = approx 150m (164yd))

**DIFFICULTY**
Intermediate

**SIZES**
XS(S:M:L:XL:XXL)
See garment measurements to check sizing

**GARMENT MEASUREMENTS**
Chest approx 92(99:106:113:120:127)cm (36¼(39:41¾:44½:47¼:50)in)
Length approx 59(61:63:65:67:69)cm (23¼(24:24¾:25½:26½:27¼)in)
Sleeve length approx 49(49:50:50:51:51)cm (19¼(19¼:19¾:19¾:20:20)in)

**YARN AMOUNT**
Yarn A: 6(7:7:8:9:10) balls
Yarn B: 3(3:3:4:4:4) balls

**SHADES USED IN VERSION SHOWN**
Yarn A: Light beige 605
Yarn B: Dark brown 603

**SUGGESTED NEEDLES**
5mm (UK 6, US 8) and 6mm (UK 4, US 10) long and short circular needles and dpns. Change from long to short circular needle and to dpns as number of sts and diameter of work decreases and vice versa.

> **TIP:** To ensure a good result when knitting with two or more colours, always hold yarns in the same position behind the work. Decide to keep the background colour innermost and the contrast colour outermost, for example.

**TENSION (GAUGE)**
17 sts and 21 rounds to approx 10cm (4in) over stocking (stockinette) stitch using 6mm (UK 4, US 10) needles. Remember that you need to maintain an even tension for a successful result. Check your tension by knitting a test swatch. Count the number of stitches per 10cm (4in). If you have more stitches than stated, go up a needle size. If you have fewer stitches, switch to smaller needles.

> **TIP:** The tension will be tighter when working the Fair Isle pattern and it is often useful to go up 0.5mm or 1mm in needle size (one or two UK/US sizes).

## BODY

Option 1 is worked in the round all the way up without dividing for armholes. Option 2 divides into front and back (each worked flat) at armholes.

### Option 1 and Option 2

Cast on 156(168:180:192:204:216) sts using 5mm (UK 6, US 8) circular needle and yarn A.
Work k2, p2 rib in stripe patt: *work 2 rounds using yarn A, 2 rounds using yarn B* (cast on counts as round 1). Rep from * to * twice for all sizes.
Change to 6mm (UK 4, US 10) circular needle.
Place marker at each side, marking 78(84:90:96:102:108) sts each for front and back.
Cont in patt following chart.

### Option 1

Cont until work measures approx 59(61:63:65:67:69)cm (23¼(24:24¾:25½:26½:27¼)in).

### BACK

Place centre 34(34:36:36:38:38) sts for back on holder for neck. Place rem 22(25:27:30:32:35) shoulder sts on each side of back on holders.

### FRONT

Place 22(25:27:30:32:35) shoulder sts on each side of front on holders.
Using tacking/basting thread, mark a neat curve for neck opening approx 6(6:6:7:7:7)cm (2½(2½:2½:2¾:2¾:2¾)in) deep between the shoulder sts. Knit sleeves.

### Option 2

When body measures 41(42:43:44:45:46)cm (16¼(16½:17:17¼:17¾:18)in) from cast on edge, divide and work each side separately.

### BACK

Cont back and forth in patt as before apart from 1 edge stitch at each side which is always knit. When work measures 59(61:63:65:67:69)cm (23¼(24:24¾:25½:26½:27¼)in), cast (bind) off centre 34(34:36:36:38:38) sts for neck. Place rem 22(25:27:30:32:35) shoulder sts on each side of back on holders.

### FRONT

Cont back and forth as for back until work measures 53(55:57:58:60:62)cm (20¾(21¾:22½:22¾:23½:24½)in). Cast (bind) off centre 18(18:20:20:22:22) sts for neck and work each side of front separately. Cont back and forth in patt as before, at the same time casting (binding) off 3, 2, 1, 1, 1 sts at neck edge on alt rows. 22(25:27:30:32:35) rem shoulder sts.
Cont until work measures 59(61:63:65:67:69)cm (23¼(24:24¾:25½:26½:27¼)in). Place sts on a holder. Work other side the same way, reversing neck shaping.

### SLEEVES
### Option 1 and Option 2

Cast on 32(32:36:36:40:44) sts using 5mm (UK 6, US 8) dpns and yarn A. Work rib in the round as for body. Change to 6mm (UK 4, US 10) needles. Place marker at beg of round = centre underarm. Count out from centre sleeve to determine start of pattern and work patt as shown in chart.
At the same time, on round 2, inc 1 st each side of marker. Rep increases approx every 2.5cm (1in) in all sizes until you have worked increase round 16(17:17:18:18:17) times in total. 64(66:70:72:76:78) rem sts.

Cont until sleeve measures 49(49:50:50:51:51)cm (19¼ (19¼:19¾:19¾:20:20)in) or desired length. End with 1 round using yarn A.

## Option 1
Turn work with WS facing and work 5 rows back and forth in stocking (stockinette) stitch to form facing. Cast (bind) off loosely.

## Option 2
Cast (bind) off loosely.

## MAKING UP
### Option 1
Stitch down each side of body with a tacking/basting thread the same length as the width of the sleeve. Using a sewing machine and its smallest zigzag stitch setting, sew two seams down each side of the tacking/basting thread for arm opening. Cut between the seams. Sew one seam using normal zigzag stitch across the cut edges.
Graft or sew together at shoulders. Sleeves will be attached after neckband.

### Option 2
Graft or sew together at shoulders.

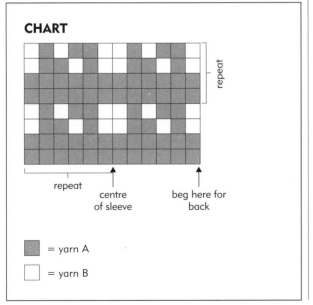

**CHART**

repeat

repeat    centre    beg here for
          of sleeve    back

█ = yarn A

☐ = yarn B

## NECKBAND
### Option 1
Knit sts from neck using 5mm (UK 6, US 8) circular needle and yarn A and pick up approx 8–9 sts per 5cm (2in) around outside of tacking/basting thread at neck edge. Number of sts must be divisible by 4. Work rib and stripe patt in the round as for body and sleeves until neckband measures approx 17cm (6¾in). End with 1 round using yarn A.
Cast (bind) off loosely in rib.
Using a sewing machine and the smallest zigzag stitch setting, sew two seams along inside of tacking/basting thread for neck opening. Cut off excess knitting. Sew using normal zigzag stitch across the cut edges. If desired, sew bias tape over edge of seam and on inside of neck.
Fold neck over to RS.
Graft or sew in sleeves. Sew down facing over cut edge.

### Option 2
Knit sts from neck using 5mm (UK 6, US 8) circular needle and yarn A and pick up approx 8–9 sts per 5cm (2in) around neck edge. Number of sts must be divisible by 4. Work rib and stripe patt in the round as for body and sleeves until neckband measures approx 17cm (6¾in). End with 1 round using yarn A.
Cast (bind) off loosely in rib.
Fold neck over to RS.
Graft or sew in sleeves.

# SAGA SWEATER
## CHILDREN

A fabulous sweater for games in the forest or in the playground.

**YARN**
Gann Garn Sky (62% baby alpaca, 16% acrylic, 22% nylon, 50g (1¾oz) = approx 150m (164yd))

**DIFFICULTY**
Intermediate

**SIZES**
Age 2–4(6:8–10:12)
See garment measurements to check sizing.

**GARMENT MEASUREMENTS**
Chest approx 63(71:78:85)cm (24¾(28:30¾:33½)in)
Length approx 38(44:52:56)cm (15(17¼:20½:22)in)
Sleeve length approx 26(33:37:40)cm
(10¼(13:14½:15¾)in)

**YARN AMOUNT**
Yarn A: 3(3:4:4) balls
Yarn B: 1(2:2:2) balls

**SHADES USED IN VERSIONS SHOWN**
Yarn A: Dark petrol 612
Yarn B: Cognac 604
(Alternative colourway: Natural 601 and Denim 614, page 97)

**SUGGESTED NEEDLES**
5mm (UK 6, US 8) and 6mm (UK 4, US 10) circular needles and dpns

**TENSION (GAUGE)**
17 sts and 21 rounds to approx 10cm (4in) over stocking (stockinette) stitch using 6mm (UK 4, US 10) needles. Remember that you need to maintain an even tension for a successful result. Check your tension by knitting a test swatch. Count the number of stitches per 10cm (4in). If you have more stitches than stated, go up a needle size. If you have fewer stitches, switch to smaller needles.

> **TIP:** The tension will be tighter when working the Fair Isle pattern and it is often useful to go up 0.5mm or 1mm in needle size (one or two UK/US sizes).

## BODY

Cast on 108(120:132:144) sts using 5mm (UK 6, US 8) circular needle and yarn A. Work k2, p2 rib in stripe patt: *work 1 round using yarn B, work 1 round using yarn A*. Rep from * to * until rib measures approx 4(4:5:5)cm (1½(1½:2:2)in) ending with 1 round using yarn A.

Change to 6mm (UK 4, US 10) needles.

Place marker at each side, marking 54(60:66:72) sts each for front and back.

Cont in patt following chart.

When work measures 23(28:34:37)cm (9(11:13½: 14½)in) from cast on edge, cast (bind) off 6(8:10:10) sts at each side for armhole, 3(4:5:5) sts either side of markers. 48(52:56:62) rem sts on each side.

Set work aside while you work sleeves.

## SLEEVES

Cast on 24(28:28:32) sts using 5mm (UK 6, US 8) dpns and yarn A. Work rib and stripe patt in the round as for body. Change to 6mm (UK 4, US 10) needles. Place marker at beg of round = centre underarm.

Count from centre sleeve on chart to determine start of pattern and work patt as shown in chart. At the same time, on round 1, inc 6(6:8:8) sts evenly across round. 30(34:36:40) rem sts.

On round 6, inc 1 st each side of marker. Then rep increase every 3(4:3.5:3.5)cm (1(1½:1⅜:1⅜)in) until you have worked increase round 7(7:9:9) times in total. 44(48:54:58) rem sts.

When sleeve measures 26(33:37:40)cm (10¼(13:14½:15¾)in) or desired length, cast (bind) off 6(8:10:10) sts at centre underarm for armhole, 3(4:5:5) sts each side of marker. 38(40:44:48) rem sts. Make sure last round of sleeve is the same chart row as last round on body.

Set aside and work other sleeve the same way.

## YOKE

Place all pieces on the same 6mm (UK 4, US 10) circular needle with one sleeve positioned over each set of cast (bound) off sts on body. 172(184:200:220) sts. Place marker in first and last st of each sleeve. 4 sts marked in round.

Cont in patt as shown in chart on each section as before. At the same time, on round 2(3:5:3) dec for raglan at each marker using yarn A: work until 2 sts before marked st, sl1 loosely, k1, psso, k1 (marked st), k2tog. 8 sts decreased across round. Rep decreases on alt rounds adapting patt on each section at decreases. At the same time, when working round 9(10:11:13) of raglan decreases, cast (bind) off 8(10:12:14) sts at centre front for neck. Work to end of round.

Beg next row at left side of neck and cont back and forth in patt as before. At the same time cast (bind) off at each side of neck edge on alt rows as foll: 2, 2, 1, 1 sts while continuing to decrease for raglan. Cont until you have worked raglan decrease round 13(14:15:17) times in total. 48(50:56:58) rem sts.

## NECKBAND

Beg at back at left shoulder using 5mm (UK 6, US 8) circular needle and yarn A. Knit sts around neck and shoulders and pick up approx 8 sts per 5cm (2in) around neck. Number of sts must be divisible by 4 and the same on each side of neck.

Work 5 rounds in rib and stripe patt as for body and sleeve cuffs. Cont using yarn A and work 6 more rounds in rib. Cast (bind) off loosely in rib.

## MAKING UP

Fold neck edge over to WS and sew down loosely. Graft or sew together at underarms.

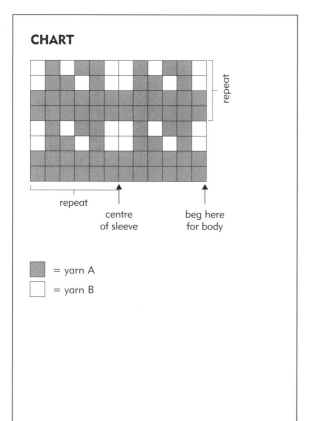

## CHART

repeat

centre
of sleeve

beg here
for body

■ = yarn A
□ = yarn B

# STYLISH
# KNITWEAR

# SUNBURST SWEATER
## WOMEN

A sweater to shine in, designed with beautiful cables radiating down over the shoulders.

**YARN**
Gann Garn Tweed (80% wool, 20% polyamide, 50g (1¾oz) = approx 112m (122yd)

**DIFFICULTY**
Experienced

**SIZES**
XS(S:M:L:XL:XXL)
See garment measurements to check sizing

**GARMENT MEASUREMENTS**
Chest approx 90(98:108:116:124:130)cm
(35½(38½:42½:45½:48½:48¾:51)in)
Length approx 56(58:60:62:64:66)cm
(22(22¾:23½:24½:25¼:26)in)
Sleeve length approx 48cm (19in) or desired length

**YARN AMOUNT**
8(9:10:11:12:13) balls

**SHADE USED IN VERSION SHOWN**
Light beige 909

**SUGGESTED NEEDLES**
4mm (UK 8, US 6) and 5mm (UK 6, US 8) long and short circular needles and dpns. Change from short to long circular needle and to dpns as number of sts and diameter of work decreases and vice versa.

**TENSION (GAUGE)**
17 sts and 24 rounds to approx 10cm (4in) over stocking (stockinette) stitch using 5mm (UK 6, US 8) needles. Remember that you need to maintain an even tension for a successful result. Check your tension by knitting a test swatch. Count the number of stitches per 10cm (4in). If you have more stitches than stated, go up a needle size. If you have fewer stitches, switch to smaller needles.

**IMPORTANT NOTE**
This sweater is knitted from the top down.

**NECK AND YOKE**
Cast on 88(90:98:106:110:116) sts using 4mm (UK 8, US 6) circular needle. Work in twisted rib (k1TBL, p1) in the round until work measures approx 6cm (2½in). Neckband will be folded over at the end.

Change to 5mm (UK 6, US 8) circular needle. Work 1 round in stocking (stockinette) stitch, increasing evenly across round to 95(100:110:120:130:135) sts. Cont in the round in patt following chart, increasing as shown. (240:264:288:312:324) sts. Once you have worked to end of chart, work 1(3:5:7:9:9) rounds in stocking (stockinette) stitch. On last stocking (stockinette) stitch round increase evenly across round to 228(250:272:294:316:332) sts
Divide work: starting from beg of round, work 66(73:82:89:96:112) sts (back), place next 48(52:54:58:62:64) sts on holder for sleeve, cast on 10 sts (underarm), work 66(73:82:89:96:112) sts (front), place next 48(52:54:58:62:64) sts on holder for other sleeve, cast on 10 sts (underarm). Cont to work body as below.

## BODY
152(166:184:198:212:224) sts. Cont in stocking (stockinette) stitch in the round until work measures approx 31(32:33:34:35:36)cm (12¼(12½:13:13½:13¾:14¼)in) from division for sleeves. Change to 4mm (UK 8, US 6) circular needle and work twisted rib (k1TBL, p1) until rib measures approx 5cm (2in) in all sizes. Cast (bind) off.

## SLEEVES
Using 5mm (UK 6, US 8) circular needle, work sts from holder for sleeve and cast on 10 new sts at underarm. 58(62:64:68:72:74) rem sts. Work in stocking (stockinette) stitch in the round until work measures approx 5cm (2in) before desired length. On last round, dec evenly across round to 34(34:36:36:38:38) sts. Change to 4mm (UK 8, US 6) dpns and work twisted rib (k1TBL, p1) until rib measures approx 5cm (2in) in all sizes. Cast (bind) off. Work other sleeve the same way.

## MAKING UP
Fold neck edge over to WS and sew down loosely. Sew together at underarms. Weave in all loose ends on WS.

# CHART

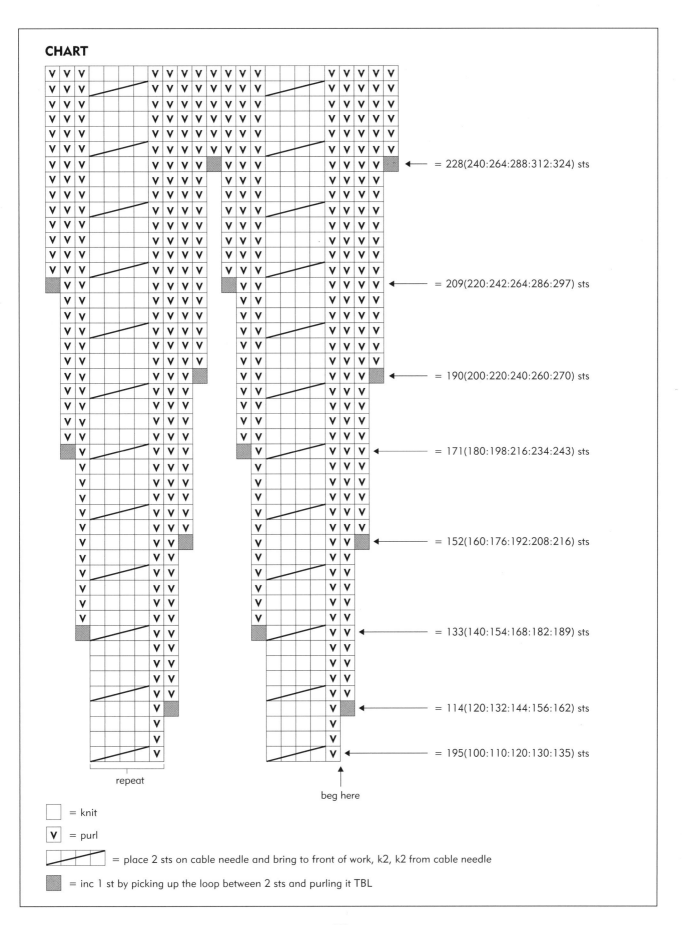

← = 228(240:264:288:312:324) sts

← = 209(220:242:264:286:297) sts

← = 190(200:220:240:260:270) sts

← = 171(180:198:216:234:243) sts

← = 152(160:176:192:208:216) sts

← = 133(140:154:168:182:189) sts

← = 114(120:132:144:156:162) sts

← = 195(100:110:120:130:135) sts

repeat

beg here

☐ = knit

V = purl

⟋ = place 2 sts on cable needle and bring to front of work, k2, k2 from cable needle

▨ = inc 1 st by picking up the loop between 2 sts and purling it TBL

# MOONLIGHT SWEATER

The pattern flows like a waterfall down the chest and back of this handsome, medium-weight sweater.

**YARN**
Gann Garn Tweed (80% wool, 20% polyamide, 50g (1¾oz) = approx 112m (122yd))

**DIFFICULTY**
Experienced

**SIZES**
S(M:L:XL:XXL:LASSE)
See garment measurements to check sizing.

**GARMENT MEASUREMENTS**
Chest approx 98(107:116:124:135:130)cm
(38½(42¼:45½:48¾:53:51)in)
Length approx 66(68:70:72:74:78)cm
(26(26¾:27½:28¼:29¼:30¾)in)
Sleeve length approx 55(56:56:57:57:60)cm
(21¾(22:22:22½:22½:23½)in)

**YARN AMOUNT**
11(12:13:14:15:15) balls

**SHADE USED IN VERSION SHOWN**
Beige 909

**SUGGESTED NEEDLES**
4.5mm (UK 7, US 7) and 5mm (UK 6, US 8) long and short circular needles and dpns. Change from long to short circular needle and to dpns as number of sts and diameter of work decreases and vice versa.

**TENSION (GAUGE)**
17 sts and 24 rounds to approx 10cm (4in) over stocking (stockinette) stitch using 5mm (UK 6, US 8) needles.
22 sts to approx 9cm (3½in) over pattern using 5mm (UK 6, US 8) needles.
Remember that you need to maintain an even tension for a successful result. Check your tension by knitting a test swatch. Count the number of stitches per 10cm (4in) or measurement specified. If you have more stitches than stated, go up a needle size. If you have fewer stitches, switch to smaller needles.

## BODY

Cast on 166(182:198:210:230:222) sts using 4.5mm (UK 7, US 7) circular needle. Work 6cm (2½in) in twisted rib (k1TBL, p1) in the round for all sizes. Change to 5mm (UK 6, US 8) circular needle. Place marker at beg of round for left side. *Work 29(33:37:39:45:43) sts in patt A following chart, p5, inc 6 sts over next 16 sts = 22 sts for patt B, p5, work 28(32:36:40:44:42) sts in patt A.* 89(97:105:111:121:117) rem sts. Place marker for right side. Rep from * to * to end of round. 178(194:210:222:242:234) sts. Cont as set without increasing until work measures approx 44(45:46:47:48:52)cm (17¼(17¾:18:18½:19: 20½)in) from cast on edge.
Divide work at each side marker and work back and front separately.

## BACK

Work back and forth in patt as before apart from 1 edge stitch at each side which is always worked as a knit st. At the same time, decrease on each side for armhole at beg of each round as follows: 2, 1, 1 sts. 81(89:97:103: 113:109) rem sts.
Cont until work measures 64(66:68:70:72:76)cm (25¼(26:26¾:27¼:28¼:30)in).
On foll row, cast (bind) off centre 37(37:39:39:41:41) sts for neck and work each side separately. Cont back and forth as set, at the same time dec 1 st at neck edge on alt rows until there are 17(21:24:27:31:29) rem shoulder sts. Cont until work measures 66(68:70:72:74:78)cm (26(26¾:27½:28¼:29¼:30¾)in). Place sts on a holder.
Work other side the same way, reversing shaping.

## FRONT

Work back and forth and shape armhole as for back. 81(89:97:103:113:109) rem sts.
Cont until work measures 59(61:63:64:66:70)cm (23¼(24:24¾:25¼:26:27½)in) at the same time decreasing 6 sts evenly across patt B on last row. On foll row cast (bind) off centre 17(17:19:19:21:21) sts for neck. Work each side separately.

Work back and forth as set, at the same time decreasing 5, 3, 2, 1, 1, st at neck edge on alt rows. 17(21:24:27:31:29) rem shoulder sts. Cont until work measures 66(68:70:72:74:78)cm (26(26¾:27½:28¼:29¼:30¾)in). Place sts on a holder.
Work other side the same way, reversing shaping.

## SLEEVES

Cast on 36(36:38:38:40:42) sts using 4mm (UK 8, US 6) dpns. Work 6cm (2in) in twisted rib (k1TBL, p1) in the round.
Change to 5mm (UK 6, US 8) circular needle. Knit 1 round increasing 8(10:10:12:12:12) sts evenly across round to 44(46:48:50:52:54) sts.
Place marker at beg of round = centre underarm. Cont in stocking (stockinette) stitch. At the same time, on second round, inc 1 st each side of marker. Rep increases approx every 3(3:2.5:2.5:2.5:3)cm (1¼(1¼:1:1:1: 1¼)in) until you have worked increase round 15(16:17:18:18:18) times in total. 74(78:82:86:88:90) rem sts.
When sleeve measures approx 55(56:56:57:57:60)cm (21¾(22:22:22½:22½:23½)in) or desired length, divide work at centre underarm. Cont back and forth in stocking (stockinette) stitch, at the same time decreasing at beg of each row as follows: 2, 1, 1 st. Cast (bind) off. Knit other sleeve the same way.

## MAKING UP

Graft or sew together at shoulders.

## NECKBAND

Beg at the back with right shoulder. Work or pick up along back and front neck approx 8 sts per 5cm (2in) using 5mm (UK 6, US 8) needles. Number of sts must be divisible by 2. Work 6cm (2½ in) in twisted rib (k1TBL, p1) in the round. Cast (bind) off loosely in rib. Fold neck edge over to WS and sew down loosely. Graft or sew in sleeves.

## CHART

PATTERN A

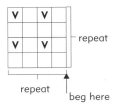

repeat

repeat

beg here

☐ = knit (knit on RS, purl on WS)

V = purl (purl on RS, knit on WS)

PATTERN B = 22 sts

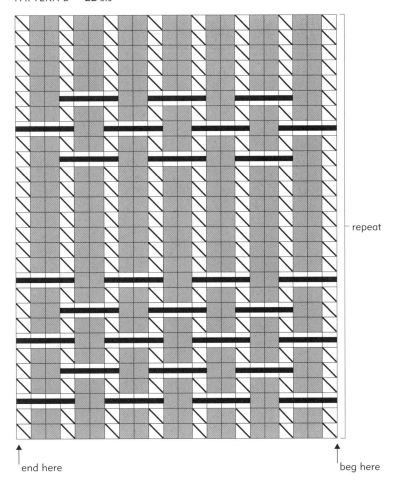

repeat

end here

beg here

◹ = knit TBL on RS, purl TBL on WS

▨ = purl on RS, knit on WS

▬▬▬ = place 4 sts on a cable needle and bring to front of
work, wrap yarn twice round the 4 sts bringing yarn
forward from back, slip 4 sts onto right-hand needle
without working them

# KNIGHT JACKET

This is a lovely jacket-cardigan I wear at all times of day – from the early hours when I'm grabbing my morning coffee, to the evening when I'm going out for dinner. The cable texture gives it a bit of heftiness, too.

**YARN**
Gann Garn Sky (62% baby alpaca, 16% acrylic, 22% nylon, 50g (1¾oz) = approx 150m (164yd))

**DIFFICULTY**
Intermediate

**SIZES**
S(M:L:XL:XXL:LASSE)
See garment measurements to check sizing.

**GARMENT MEASUREMENTS**
Chest approx 105(113:121:129:140:140)cm
(41½(44½:47¾:50¾:55½:55¼)in)
Length approx 78(80:82:84:86:90)cm
(30¾(31½:32¼:33:33¾:35½)in)
Sleeve length approx 50(50:52:54:56:58)cm
(19¾(19¾:20½:21¼:22: 22¾)in)

**YARN AMOUNT**
12(13:13:14:15:15) balls

**SHADE USED IN VERSION SHOWN**
Grey melange 607

**SUGGESTED NEEDLES**
4.5mm (UK 7, US 7) and 5mm (UK 6, US 8) long and short circular needles and dpns. Change from long to short circular needle and to dpns as number of sts and diameter of work decreases and vice versa.

**TENSION (GAUGE)**
20 sts and 25 rounds to approx 10cm (4in) over pattern using 6mm (UK 4, US 10) needles. Remember that you need to maintain an even tension for a successful result. Check your tension by knitting a test swatch. Count the number of stitches per 10cm (4in). If you have more stitches than stated, go up a needle size. If you have fewer stitches, switch to smaller needles.

## BODY

Cast on 221(237:253:269:293:293) sts using 5mm (UK 6, US 8) circular needle. Working back and forth work approx 5cm (2in) in k1, p1 rib for all sizes. Change to 6mm (UK 4, US 10) circular needle. Place first 10 and last 10 sts on a holder. These are for the front bands which are worked at the end. Purl 1 row from WS, increasing 1 st. Place marker at sides marking 49(52:57:61:67:67) sts for each front and 104(114:120:128:140:140) sts for back. Work back and forth in patt following chart. Beg and end with 1 edge st. Knit this edge st on all rows. Cont until work measures approx 55(56:57:58:59:63)cm (21¾(22:22½:22¾:23¼:24¾)in). Divide work at side markers and work fronts and back separately.

## BACK

Work back and forth in patt as set. Cont until work measures 78(80:82:84:86:90)cm (30¾(31½:32¼:33:33¾:35½)in) and armhole measures approx 23(24:25:26:27:27)cm (9(9½:9¾:10¼:10¾:10¾)in). Cast (bind) off.

## FRONTS

Work fronts separately, starting with right front. Work back and forth in patt as before. At the same time, dec for V-neck on every fourth row by working k2tog at beg of RS row. Cont until you have decreased 15(15:16:16:17:18:18) times in total. 33(37:40:43:48:48) rem sts for shoulder. Work until front is the same length as back. Cast (bind) off. Work left front the same way but working k2tog at end of RS row.

## SLEEVES

Cast on 36(38:40:40:42:44) sts using 5mm (UK 6, US 8) dpns. Work 5cm (2in) in k1, p1 rib in the round. Change to 6mm (UK 4, US 10) needles and knit 1 round increasing evenly across round to 60(64:66:70:72:76) sts. Place marker at beg of round = centre underarm. Count out from centre to determine start of patt and work in the round in patt following chart at the same time increasing 1 st each side of marker approx every 2.5(2.5:2.5:2.5:2.5:3)cm (1(1:1:1:1:1¼)in) until there are 92(96:100:104:108:108) sts. Work until sleeve measures stated or desired length. Cast (bind) off.

## MAKING UP

Sew together at shoulders.

## FRONT BANDS

Move sts on holder for left front band on to 5mm (UK 6, US 8) needle. Work in rib back and forth until front band reaches centre back at neck. Gently stretch work while measuring. Place sts on a holder or cast (bind) off.
Work right front band the same way.
Graft or sew front bands together at centre back neck and sew them down to back and V-neck/fronts on both sides.
Sew in sleeves.

## CHART

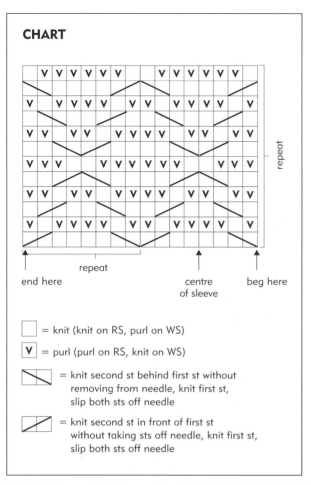

repeat

repeat

end here          centre          beg here
                 of sleeve

☐ = knit (knit on RS, purl on WS)

V = purl (purl on RS, knit on WS)

⬚ = knit second st behind first st without removing from needle, knit first st, slip both sts off needle

⬚ = knit second st in front of first st without taking sts off needle, knit first st, slip both sts off needle

# QUEEN COATIGAN
## WOMEN

If the Knight Jacket is dashing, this one is truly elegant.
Queen Coatigan is attractive to wear, with decorative balloon
sleeves and chunky cables.

**YARN**
Gann Garn Sky (62% baby alpaca, 16% acrylic,
22% nylon, 50g (1¾oz) = approx 150m (164yd))

**DIFFICULTY**
Experienced

**SIZES**
S(M:L:XL:XXL)
See garment measurements to check sizing

**GARMENT MEASUREMENTS**
Chest approx 105(113:121:129:140)cm
(41½(44½:47½:50¾:55¼)in)
Length approx 88(90:92:94:96)cm
(34¾(35½:36¼:37:37¾)in)
Sleeve length approx 48(49:49:50:50)cm
(19(19¼:19¼:19¾:19¾)in)

**YARN AMOUNT**
14(15:16:17:18) balls

**SHADE USED IN VERSION SHOWN**
Cognac 604

**SUGGESTED NEEDLES**
5mm (UK 6, US 8) and 6mm (UK 4, US 10) long and
short circular needles and dpns. Change from long
to short circular needle and to dpns as number of sts
and diameter of work decreases and vice versa.

**TENSION (GAUGE)**
20 sts and 26 rounds to approx 10cm (4in) over
pattern using 6mm (UK 4, US 10) needles.
Remember that you need to maintain an even tension
for a successful result. Check your tension by knitting
a test swatch. Count the number of stitches per 10cm
(4in). If you have more stitches than stated, go up
a needle size. If you have fewer stitches, switch to
smaller needles.

**BODY**
Cast on 221(237:253:269:293) sts using 5mm (UK 6,
US 8) circular needle. Working back and forth work
approx 5cm (2in) in k1, p1 rib for all sizes. Change
to 6mm (UK 4, US 10) circular needle. Place first 10
and last 10 sts on a holder. These are for the front
bands which will be worked at the end. Purl 1 row
from WS and inc 1 st at end of row. Place marker at
each side, marking 49(53:57:61:67) sts for each front
and 104(112:120:128:140) sts for back. Work back
and forth in patt following chart but always working
first and last st on needle as a knit stitch. These are
edge stitches. Cont until work measures approx
65(65:67:69:68)cm (25½(25½:26½:27¼:26¾)in).
Divide work at side markers and work front and
back separately.

**BACK**
Work back and forth in patt as before and at the same
time inc 1 st at beg and 1 st at end of row. These are

edge stitches and are always worked as knit stitches.
Cont until work measures 88(90:92:94:96)cm
(34¾(35½:36¼:37:37¾)in) and armhole measures
approx 23(25:25:25:28)cm (9(9¾:9¾:9¾:11)in).
Cast (bind) off.

## FRONTS

Work fronts separately, working back and forth in
patt as before. For right front, dec for V-neck on every
fourth row by working k2togTBL at beg of RS row.
Cont until you have decreased 15(15:16:16:17:18)
times in total. 34(38:41:44:49) rem sts for shoulder.
Work until front is the same length as back.
Cast (bind) off.
Work left front the same way reversing shaping,
decreasing for V-neck at end of RS row by working
until 3 sts rem, k2tog, k1 (edge st).

## SLEEVES

Cast on 32(36:36:36:40) sts using 5mm (UK 6,
US 8) dpns. Work 5cm (2in) in k1, p1 rib in the
round. Change to 6mm (UK 4, US 10) needles and
knit 2 rounds. On first round inc 1 st in each st to
64(72:72:72:80) sts, and on second round inc to a
total 126(140:140:140:154) sts in round. Next work
in cable patt following chart until sleeve measures
stated or desired length. Cast (bind) off.

## MAKING UP

Sew together at shoulders.

## FRONT BANDS

Place sts on holder for left front band onto 5mm (UK 6,
US 8) needle. Work in rib back and forth until front
band reaches around neck to centre back. Gently
stretch work while measuring. Place sts on a holder.
Work right front band the same way.
Graft or sew front bands together at centre back neck
and sew to back neck, down V-neck and to fronts on
both sides
Sew in sleeves.

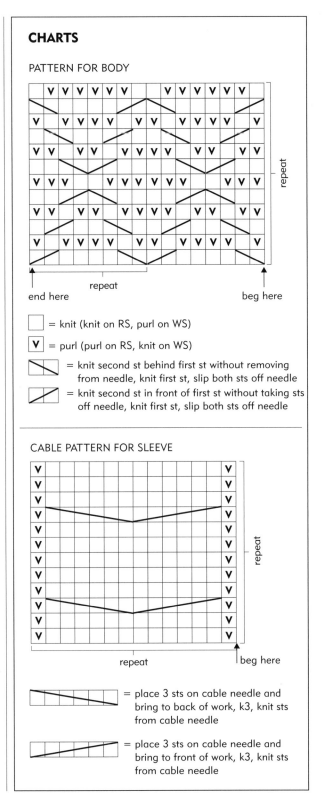

**CHARTS**

PATTERN FOR BODY

repeat

end here          repeat          beg here

☐ = knit (knit on RS, purl on WS)

Ⅴ = purl (purl on RS, knit on WS)

◹ = knit second st behind first st without removing
from needle, knit first st, slip both sts off needle

◹ = knit second st in front of first st without taking sts
off needle, knit first st, slip both sts off needle

CABLE PATTERN FOR SLEEVE

repeat

repeat          beg here

◹ = place 3 sts on cable needle and
bring to back of work, k3, knit sts
from cable needle

◹ = place 3 sts on cable needle and
bring to front of work, k3, knit sts
from cable needle

# WAVE SWEATER

The small cables on this sweater make a fabulous wave pattern. As well as fitting comfortably, this sweater uses a finer yarn that makes it light and breathable. This is a sound summer sweater.

**YARN**
Gann Garn Myk Merino (100% superwash merino wool, 50g (1¾oz) = approx 120m (131yd))

**DIFFICULTY**
Intermediate

**SIZES**
S(M:L:XL:XXL:LASSE)
See garment measurements to check sizing

**GARMENT MEASUREMENTS**
Chest approx 98(104:114:121:125:125)cm
(38½(41:44¾:47¾:49¼:49¼)in)
Length approx 66(68:70:72:74:76)cm
(26(26¾:27½:28¼:29¼:30)in)
Sleeve length approx 52(52:54:56:56:60)cm
(20½(20½:21¼:22:22:23½)in)

**YARN AMOUNT**
14(15:16:17:18:18) balls

**SHADE USED IN VERSION SHOWN**
Navy 715

**SUGGESTED NEEDLES**
3.5mm (UK 9/10, US 4) and 4.5mm (UK 7, US 7) long and short circular needles and dpns. Change from long to short circular needle and to dpns as number of sts and diameter of work decreases and vice versa.

**TENSION (GAUGE)**
22 sts and 28 rounds to approx 10cm (4in) over stocking (stockinette) stitch using 4.5mm (UK 7, US 7) needles. Remember that you need to maintain an even tension for a successful result. Check your tension by knitting a test swatch. Count the number of stitches per 10cm (4in). If you have more stitches than stated, go up a needle size. If you have fewer stitches, switch to smaller needles.

**BODY**

Cast on 216(228:252:264:276:276) sts using 3.5mm (UK 9/10, US 4) circular needle. Work approx 6cm (2½in) in k1, p1 rib in the round for all sizes. Change to 4.5mm (UK 7, US 7) circular needle. Place marker at each side, marking 108(114:126:132:138:138) sts each for front and back. Work in the round in patt following chart. For sizes S and XL, which start mid-cable, count back 2 sts onto the back and beg the cable from there. Work following chart until body measures approx 44(45:46: 47:48:50)cm (17¼(17¾:18:18½:19:19¾)in).
Divide work at side markers and work front and back separately.

**BACK**

Work back and forth in patt as before. For sizes S and XL, which now beg/end mid-cable, cont working these sts in stocking (stockinette) stitch with no cable. Cont until work measures 66(68:70:72:74:76)cm (26(26¾:27½:28¼:29¼:30)in) and armhole measures approx 22(23:24:25:26:26)cm (8¾(9:9½:9¾:10¼:10¼)in). Cast (bind) off.

**FRONT**

Work as for back but when armhole measures approx 7(8:9:10:11:11)cm (2¾(3¼:3½:4:4¼:4¼)in), cast (bind) off centre 22(24:24:26:26:28) sts for neck. Make sure you cast (bind) off so that cables continue on RS. Work each side separately and dec for neck as foll: dec 1 st before first st by working k2togTBL on right front and k2tog on left front. Dec in this way on every fourth row 10 times in total for all sizes. Work until front is the same length as back. Cast (bind) off.

**SLEEVES**

Cast on 48(48:52:52:56) sts using 3.5mm (UK 9/10, US 4) dpns. Work 6cm (2½in) in k1, p1 rib in the round. Change to 4.5mm needles (UK 7, US 7) and knit 1 round increasing evenly across round to 64(66:70:72:76:76) sts. Place marker at beg of round = centre underarm. Work in the round following patt as shown in chart at the same time increasing 1 st each side of marker approx every 2.5(2.5:2.5:2.5:2.5:2.5) cm (1(1:1:1:1:1)in) to 96(102:106:110:114:114) sts in total. Work until sleeve measures stated or desired length. Cast (bind) off.

**MAKING UP**

Graft or sew together at shoulders.

**NECKBAND**

Beg at bottom of neckband on right front. Using 4.5mm (UK 7, US 7) circular needle pick up approx 12-13 sts per 5cm (2in) along vertical side of right front, round neck and along vertical side of left front. Approx 129(135:139:139:145:145) sts. Work back and forth in k1, p1 rib until neckband measures approx 12(13:13:14:14:15)cm (4¾(5:5:5½:5½:6)in). Cast (bind) off loosely in rib or using an elastic cast (bind) off (see page 163). Place one neckband flap over the other and sew both edges down along horizontal cast (bound) off edge on front.
Sew in sleeves.

## CHART

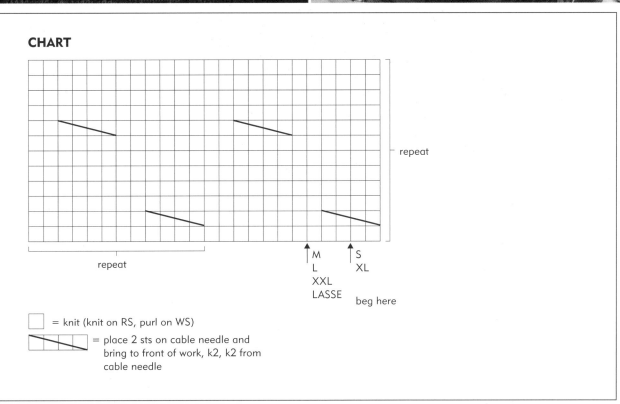

repeat

repeat

↑ M
  L
  XXL
  LASSE

↑ S
  XL

beg here

☐ = knit (knit on RS, purl on WS)

▱ = place 2 sts on cable needle and
    bring to front of work, k2, k2 from
    cable needle

# MIDSUMMER SWEATER

The wide neck and airy texture of this sweater make this perfect for the midsummer bonfire or a light summer evening in the midnight sun.

## YARN
Gann Garn Myk Merino (100% superwash merino wool, 50g (1¾oz) = approx 120m (131yd))

## DIFFICULTY
Intermediate

## SIZES
S(M:L:XL:XXL:LASSE)
See garment measurements to check sizing

## GARMENT MEASUREMENTS
Chest approx 95(103:111:119:127:127)cm (37½(40½:43¾:46¾:50:50)in)
Length approx 66(68:70:72:74:76)cm (26(26¾:27½:28¼:29¼:30)in)
Sleeve length approx 50(50:52:52:53:53)cm (19¾(19¾:20½:20½:20¾:20¾)in)

## YARN AMOUNT
16(17:18:19:20:20) balls

## SHADE USED IN VERSION SHOWN
Dark olive 711

## SUGGESTED NEEDLES
3.5mm (UK 9/10, US 4) and 4.5mm (UK 7, US 7) long and short circular needles and dpns. Change from long to short circular needle and to dpns as number of sts and diameter of work decreases and vice versa.

## NOTIONS
Two 20–25mm (¾–1in) buttons

## TENSION (GAUGE)
22 sts and 34 rows to approx 10cm (4in) over pattern using 4.5mm (UK 7, US 7) needles.
Remember that you need to maintain an even tension for a successful result. Check your tension by knitting a test swatch. Count the number of stitches per 10cm (4in). If you have more stitches than stated, go up a needle size. If you have fewer stitches, switch to smaller needles.

## BODY
Cast on 212(228:244:264:280:280) sts using 3.5mm (UK 9/10, US 4) circular needle. Work approx 6cm (2½in) in k1, p1 rib in the round for all sizes. Change to 4.5mm (UK 7, US 7) needle. Place marker at each side, marking 107(115:123:133:141:141) sts for front and 105(113:121:131:139:139) sts for back.

Work in the round in patt following chart. Cont until work measures approx 48(49:50:51:52:53)cm (19(19¼:19¾:20:20½:20¾in)). Cast (bind) off 14 sts on each side, 7 sts each side of marker. Set work aside while you knit sleeves.

## SLEEVES

Cast on 48(48:52:52:56:56) sts using 3.5mm (UK 9/10, US 4) dpns. Work 6cm (2½in) in k1, p1 rib in the round. Change to 4.5mm needles (UK 7, US 7) and knit 1 round increasing evenly across round to 62(64:66:70:72:74) sts. Place marker at beg of round = centre underarm. Work in the round in patt as shown in chart while increasing 1 st on each side of marker approx every 4.5(4:4:4:3.5:3.5)cm (1¾(1½:1½:1½:1⅜:1⅜)in) to a total 80(84:88:92:96:100) sts. Work until sleeve measures stated or desired length. Make sure to end sleeve with same round of chart as for body. Cast (bind) off 14 sts at centre underarm, 7 sts each side of marker. Set aside and knit other sleeve the same way.

## YOKE

Place all pieces on the same 4.5mm (UK 7, US 7) circular needle with one sleeve positioned over each set of cast (bound) off sts on body. 314(338:366:394:418:426) rem sts. Cont in patt as before, placing a marker at all four joins. Work until 8 sts before marker: sl1 loosely, k1, psso, work 11 sts in twisted rib (k1TBL, p1), k2tog. Work decreases at all four joins. 8 sts decreased. Dec on every alt round until you have worked raglan decrease round 13(15:17:20:22:23) times in total. Cast (bind) off centre 7 sts on front (for all sizes). Work to end of round. Break yarn and beg at centre front at neck. Check that you are starting raglan decreases on RS. Work back and forth in patt, continuing to decrease for raglan as before, until there are 22(25:27:30:32:33) raglan decreases. Dec for neck: cast (bind) off 8(10:12:13:16:15) sts once on each side, then dec on every alt row at both sides of neck

as follows: 4, 2, 2, 1 sts. Cont until you have worked 27(30:32:35:37:38) raglan decreases on back in total. Place sts on a holder.

## NECKBAND

See close-up picture on page 125. Beg at side of V-shaped neck on right front. Using 3.5mm (UK 9/10, US 4) circular needle pick up approx 12 sts per 5cm (2in) along side of right front, round neck and down side of left front. Mark 1 st at corners between sides of neckband at front and rest of neckband. Work 5 rows back and forth in k1, p1 rib while increasing 1 st on either side of marked sts on every alt row at both transitions in all sizes. Next work buttonholes on RS row. Work 3 sts in rib, cast (bind) off 2 sts which you cast back on in next row, work 7 sts in rib, cast (bind) off 2 sts which will be cast back on in next row. Cont in rib until neckband measures approx 3cm (1¼in). Cast (bind) off loosely in rib.

## MAKING UP

Sew together at underarms. Weave in all loose ends on WS. Sew on buttons. Overlap edges of neckband and sew down to cast (bound) off edge at centre front.

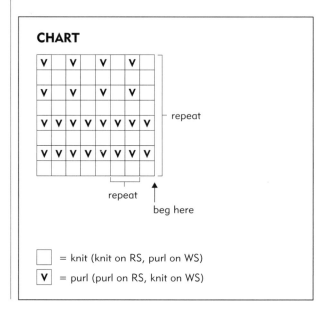

CHART

repeat

repeat

beg here

☐ = knit (knit on RS, purl on WS)

V = purl (purl on RS, knit on WS)

# PAPA SWEATER

Good, warm, reliable and robust – just like my dad. This sweater will never let you down!

**YARN**
Gann Garn Sky (62% baby alpaca, 16% acrylic, 22% nylon, 50g (1¾oz) = approx 150m (164yd))

**DIFFICULTY**
Intermediate

**SIZES**
S(M:L:XL:XXL:LASSE)
See garment measurements below to check sizing

**GARMENT MEASUREMENTS**
Chest approx 100(110:120:130:140:130)cm
(39¼(43¼:47¼:51:55½:51)in)
Length approx 66(68:70:72:74:76)cm
(26(26¾:27½:28¼:29¼:30)in)
Sleeve length approx 52(52:54:56:56:60)cm
(20½(20½:21¼:22:22:23½)in)

**YARN AMOUNT**
9(10:11:12:13:12) balls

**SHADE USED IN VERSION SHOWN**
Light grey 606

**SUGGESTED NEEDLES**
5mm (UK 6, US 8) and 6mm (UK 4, US 10) long and short circular needles and dpns. Change from long to short circular needle and to dpns as number of sts and diameter of work decreases and vice versa.

**TENSION (GAUGE)**
18 sts and 25 rows to approx 10cm (4in) over pattern using 6mm (UK 4, US 10) needles.
Remember that you need to maintain an even tension for a successful result. Check your tension by knitting a test swatch. Count the number of stitches per 10cm (4in). If you have more stitches than stated, go up a needle size. If you have fewer stitches, switch to smaller needles.

## BODY

Cast on 168(196:216:232:252:232) sts using 5mm (UK 6, US 8) circular needle. Work approx 6cm (2½in) in k2, p2 rib in the round for all sizes. Change to 6mm (UK 4, US 10) circular needle. Place marker at each side, marking 86(98:110:118:128:118) sts for front and 82(98:106:114:124:1114) sts for back. Work in the round in patt following chart. Work following chart until body measures approx 44(45:46:47:48:50)cm (17¼(17¾:18:18½:19:19¾)in) Divide work at side markers and work front and back separately.

## BACK

Work back and forth in patt as set. Cont until work measures 66(68:70:72:74:76)cm (26(26¾:27½:28¼:29¼:30)in) and armhole measures approx 22(23:24:25:26:26)cm (8¾(9:9½:9¾:10¼:10¼)in). Cast (bind) off.

## FRONT

Work as for back but when armhole measures approx 4(4:5:5:6:6)cm (1½(1½:2:2:2½:2½)in), cast (bind) off centre 18(18:20:20:22:20) sts for neck. Working each side separately, cont decreasing for neck by decreasing 1 st inside first st by k2togTBL on right front and k2tog on left front. Dec in the same way on every fourth row until you have worked decrease rows 10 times in total. 24(30:35:39:43:39) rem sts for shoulder. Work until front is the same length as back. Cast (bind) off.

## SLEEVES

Cast on 36(36:40:40:44:44) sts using 5mm (UK 6, US 8) dpns. Work 6cm (2½in) in k2, p2 rib in the round. Change to 6mm (UK 4, US 10) needles and knit 1 round increasing evenly across round to 56(60:64:68:72:72) sts. Place marker at beg of round = centre underarm. Count out from centre to determine start of patt and work in the round in patt following chart at the same time as increasing 1 st each side of marker approx every 3.5(4:4:4:4:4)cm

(1⅜(1½:1½:1½:1½:1½)in) until there are 80(82:86:90:94:94) sts. Work until sleeve measures stated or desired length. Cast (bind) off.

## MAKING UP

Sew together at shoulders.

## NECKBAND

Beg at bottom of side of neckband on right front. Using 5mm (UK 6, US 8) circular needle pick up approx 10 sts per 5cm (2in) along side of V-neck on right front, round neck and down side of V-neck on left front. Number of sts must be divisible by 4 + 2 sts. Work back and forth in k2, p2 rib until neckband measures approx 10(10:11:11:12:12)cm (4(4:4¼:4¼:4¾:4¾)in). Cast (bind) off loosely in rib. Overlap edges and sew down to cast (bind) off horizontal edge at centre front.
Sew in sleeves. Weave in all loose ends.

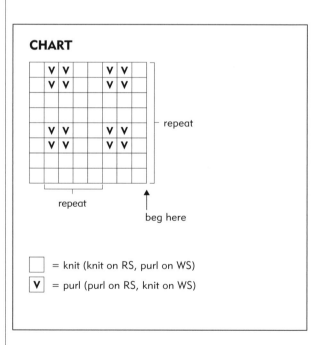

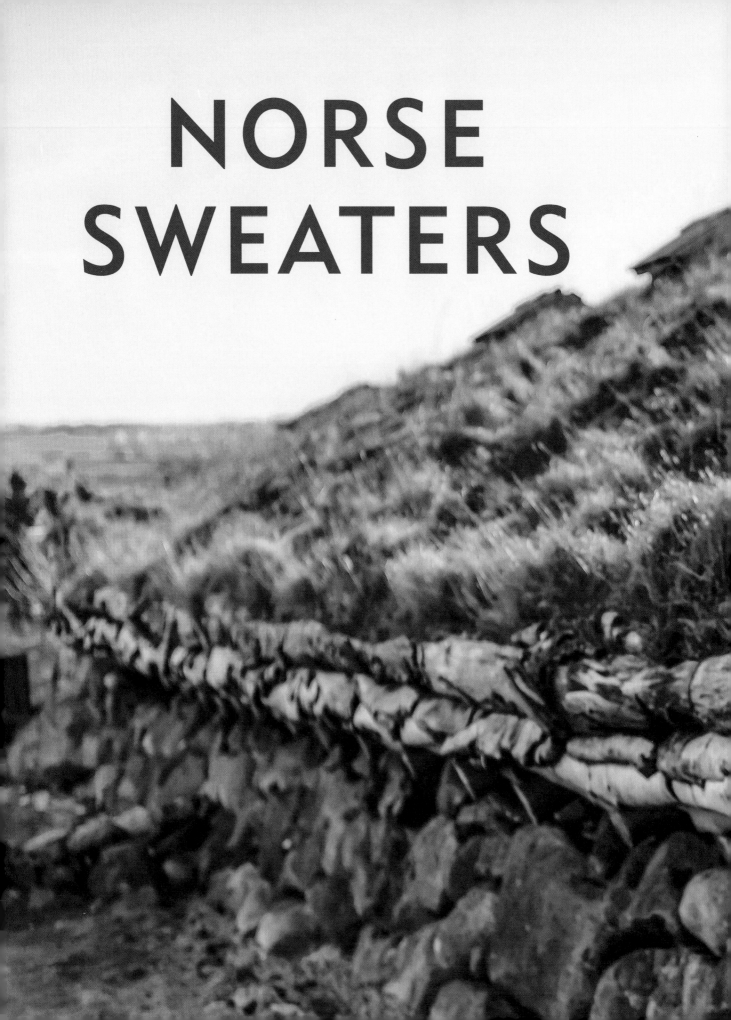

# NORSE
# SWEATERS

# THE VIKING

If you want to look as impressive as a Viking, it's got to be this sweater with a gorgeous cable pattern on the sleeve. In it, you're ready for sitting at a long table with a glass of mead followed by singing and dancing!

**YARN**
Gann Garn Tweed (80% wool, 20% polyamide, 50g (1¾oz) = approx 112m (122yd))

**DIFFICULTY**
Intermediate

**SIZES**
S(M:L:XL:XXL:LASSE)
See garment measurements below to check sizing

**GARMENT MEASUREMENTS**
Chest approx 95(102:109:116:124:124)cm (37½(40¼:43:45½:48¾:48¾)in)
Length approx 66(68:70:72:74:76)cm (26(26¾:27½:28¼:29¼:30)in)
Sleeve length approx 50(50:52:52:53:53)cm (19¾(19¾:20½:20½:20¾:20¾)in)

**YARN AMOUNT**
11(12:12:13:14:14) balls

**SHADE USED IN VERSION SHOWN**
Grey-brown 911

**SUGGESTED NEEDLES**
4mm (UK 8, US 6) and 5mm (UK 6, US 8) long and short circular needles and dpns. Change from long to short circular needle and to dpns as number of sts and diameter of work decreases and vice versa.

**TENSION (GAUGE)**
17 sts and 24 rounds to approx 10cm (4in) over stocking (stockinette) stitch using 5mm (UK 6, US 8) needles. Remember that you need to maintain an even tension for a successful result. Check your tension by knitting a test swatch. Count the number of stitches per 10cm (4in). If you have more stitches than stated, go up a needle size. If you have fewer stitches, switch to smaller needles.

## BODY

Cast on 160(176:188:200:216:216) sts using 4mm (UK 8, US 6) circular needle. Work approx 6cm (2½in) in k2, p2 rib in the round for all sizes. Change to 5mm (UK 6, US 8) circular needle. Place marker at each side, marking 80(88:94:100:108:108) each sts for front and back. Cont in stocking (stockinette) stitch in the round until work measures approx 48(49:50:51:52:54)cm (19(19¼:19¾:20:20½:21¼)in). Cast (bind) off 12 sts on each side, 6 sts each side of marker. Set work aside while you knit sleeves.

## SLEEVES

Cast on 36(36:40:40:44:44) sts using 4mm (UK 8, US 6) dpns. Work 6cm (2½in) in k2, p2 rib in the round. Change to 5mm (UK 6, US 8) needles. Knit 1 round increasing as foll: work 9(9:11:11:13:13) sts in stocking (stockinette) stitch, inc 10 sts over next 18 sts = 28 sts for patt, work 9(9:11:11:13:13) sts in stocking (stockinette) stitch. 48(48:50:50:54:54) rem sts in round. Place marker at beg of round = centre underarm. Work in the round in stocking (stockinette) stitch at sides and patt as shown in chart at centre sleeve while increasing 1 st each side of marker approx every 3.5(3:3:2.5:2.5:2.5)cm (1⅜(1¼:1¼:1:1:1)in) until there are 72(76:80:84:86:86) sts in total. Work until sleeve measures stated or desired length. Cast (bind) off 12 sts at centre underarm, 6 sts each side of marker. Set aside and work other sleeve the same way.

## YOKE

Place all pieces on the same 5mm (UK 6, US 8) circular needle with one sleeve positioned over each set of cast (bound) off sts on body. 256(280:300:320:340:340) sts. Cont in patt on sleeves and stocking (stockinette) stitch on body as set. Place marker at each join. Work until 3 sts before marker: sl1 loosely, k1, psso, k2, k2tog. Work decreases at all four joins. 8 sts decreased per round. Dec in the same way on every alt round until you have worked raglan decrease round 17(19:22:24:26:26) times in total. Note that as you continue, the raglan decreases will start to absorb the cable pattern on sleeves. On next round, cast (bind) off centre 10(14:14:16:20:20) sts on front for neck. Work to end of round. Break yarn and beg at front after cast (bound) off sts. Cont back and forth in stocking (stockinette) stitch and patt as before, continuing to dec for raglan. At the same time, cont to decrease at each side of neck on every alt row as follows: 4, 2, 1 sts. Cont until you have worked 21(23:26:28:30:30) raglan decreases on back in total. 64(68:64:66:66:66) rem sts. Work neckband.

## NECKBAND

Using 4mm circular needle (UK 8, US 6), pick up 24(28:32:34:34:34) sts at front neck. 88(96:96:100:100:100) sts in total. Work 3cm (1¼in) in k2, p2 rib in the round. Purl 1 round (forms foldline). Work 3cm (1¼in) in rib. Cast (bind) off loosely in rib. Fold edge over to WS and sew down loosely.

## MAKING UP

Sew together at underarms. Weave in all loose ends on WS.

## CHART

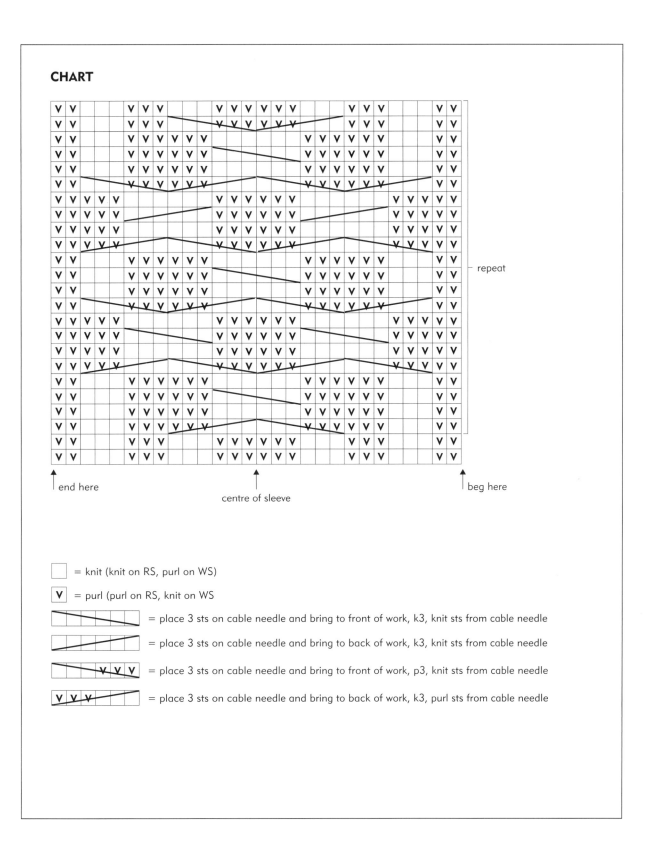

repeat

end here

centre of sleeve

beg here

☐ = knit (knit on RS, purl on WS)

V = purl (purl on RS, knit on WS

= place 3 sts on cable needle and bring to front of work, k3, knit sts from cable needle

= place 3 sts on cable needle and bring to back of work, k3, knit sts from cable needle

= place 3 sts on cable needle and bring to front of work, p3, knit sts from cable needle

= place 3 sts on cable needle and bring to back of work, k3, purl sts from cable needle

# STORM HOODIE

This hoodie is like a bivouac made of wool to retreat to in a storm. Or put it on when you stop for a rest after a hard skiing session or a winter walk. The hood is generous and the length makes this hoodie long enough to sit on.

**YARN**
Gann Garn Tweed (80% wool, 20% polyamide, 50g (1¾oz) = approx 112m (122yd))

**DIFFICULTY**
Intermediate

**SIZES**
S(M:L:XL:XXL:LASSE)
See garment measurements to check sizing

**GARMENT MEASUREMENTS**
Chest approx 105(114:121:130:140:130)cm (41½(44¾:47¾:51:55¼:51)in)
Length approx 77(79:81:83:85:88)cm (30¼(31:32:32¾:33½:34¾)in)
Sleeve length approx 50(51:52:52:53:55)cm (19¾(20:20½:20½:20¾:21¾)in)

**YARN AMOUNT**
Yarn A: 13(14:15:16:17:18) balls
Yarn B: one ball for all sizes

**SHADE USED IN VERSION SHOWN**
Yarn A: Light grey 910
Yarn B: Dark grey 908

**SUGGESTED NEEDLES**
4.5mm (UK 7, US 7) and 5mm (UK 6, US 8) long and short circular needles and dpns. Change from long to short circular needle and to dpns as number of sts and diameter of work decreases and vice versa.

**TENSION (GAUGE)**
17 sts and 24 rounds to approx 10cm (4in) over stocking (stockinette) stitch using 5mm (UK 6, US 8) needles. Remember that you need to maintain an even tension for a successful result. Check your tension by knitting a test swatch. Count the number of stitches per 10cm (4in). If you have more stitches than stated, go up a needle size. If you have fewer stitches, switch to smaller needles.

**BODY**
Cast on 178(194:206:222:238:222) sts using 4.5mm (UK 7, US 7) circular needle and yarn A. Work 7cm (2¾in) in stocking (stockinette) stitch in the round. Purl 1 round (forms foldline). Change to 5mm (UK 6, US 8) circular needle. Cont in stocking (stockinette) stitch. Place marker at each side, marking 89(97:103:111:119:111) each for front and back. When work measures 55(56:57:58:59:61)cm (21¾(22:22½:22¾:23¼:24)in) from the foldline,

cast (bind) off 12(12:12:14:14:14) sts at each side for armhole, 6(6:6:7:7:7) sts either side of markers. 77(85:91:97:105:97) rem sts on each side. Set aside while you work sleeves.

## SLEEVES

Cast on 40(42:42:44:46:46) sts using 4.5mm (UK 7, US 7) dpns and yarn B. Work 6cm (2½in) in k1, p1 rib in the round. At the same time, on fourth round, change to yarn A. Change to 5mm (UK 6, US 8) needles. Knit 1 round increasing 8 sts evenly across round to 48(50:50:52:54:54) sts.

Place marker at beg of round = centre underarm. Cont in stocking (stockinette) stitch. On third round inc 1 st each side of marker. Then rep increase every 5.5(5:4.4:4.4)cm (2¼(2:1½:1½:1½:1½)in) until you have worked increase round 8(9:11:11:11:12) times in total. 64(68:72:74:76:78) rem sts. When sleeve measures 50(51:52:52:53:55)cm (19¾(20:20½:20½:20¾:21¾)in) or desired length, cast (bind) off 12(12:12:14:14:14) sts at centre underarm for armhole, 6(6:6:7:7:7) sts each side of marker. 52(56:60:60:62:64) sts. Set aside and work other sleeve the same way.

## YOKE

Place all pieces on the same 5mm (UK 6, US 8) circular needle with one sleeve positioned over each set of cast (bound) off sts on body. 258(282:302:314:334:322) sts. Place marker at each join, four markers in round. Beg at back at right shoulder using yarn A. Knit 1 round decreasing 2(2:6:2:6:2) sts evenly across round to 256(280:296:312:328:320) sts. Work in patt following chart.

Cont in stocking (stockinette) stitch using yarn A, decreasing for raglan at the same time on round 1 as foll: at start of round k1, k2tog, *work until 3 sts before next marker, sl1 loosely, k1, psso, k2, k2tog*, rep from * to * at next two markers. Work until 3 sts before last marker, sl1 loosely, k1, psso, k1. 8 sts decreased across round. Rep raglan decreases on every round 3(4:7:8:9:5)

more times, then on alt rounds 16(17:16:16:17:20) times until you have worked 20(22:24:25:27:26) raglan decrease rounds in total. At the same time, on raglan decrease round 15(17:19:20:22:21), cast (bind) off centre 17(21:23:27:31:25) sts at front neck and work rest of round.

Break yarn. Beg at left neck edge. Cont back and forth in stocking (stockinette) stitch and working raglan decreases as before, at the same time casting (binding) off 1 st at each side of neck edge on every alt row as follows: 3, 2, 1, 1, 1 sts. 63(67:65:69:65:71) rem sts.

## NECKBAND

Beg at back at right shoulder using 4.5mm (UK 7, US 7) circular needle and yarn A. Knit sts from neck and left shoulder, pick up approx 8–9 sts per 5cm (2in) around neck edge and knit sts from right shoulder. Number of sts must be divisible by 2. Work 6cm (2½in) in k1, p1 rib in the round. Cast (bind) off loosely in rib.

Fold neck edge over to WS and sew down loosely.

## HOOD

Cast on 119(121:123:125:127:125) sts using 5mm (UK 6, US 8) circular needle and yarn B. Work 6cm (1½in) back and forth in stocking (stockinette) stitch. Change to yarn A. Cont in stocking (stockinette) stitch while decreasing 1 st at beg of each row four times. 111(113:115:117:119:117) rem sts.

Cont until work measures 34(36:38:40:40:40)cm (13½(14¼:15:15¾:15¾:15¾)in). Cast (bind) off centre 21 sts in all sizes. 45(46:47:48:49:48) sts for each half. Work 6cm (1½in) back and forth in stocking (stockinette) stitch on each side of the cast (bound) off sts. Graft the sts of each side together. This forms the centre back of the hood. Sew the end of each side section down to the cast (bound) off sts on the hood. Turn neckband over to WS and sew down as a casing. Sew hood to attach from centre back at neck to centre front on neck. Ease in the back of the hood slightly if necessary.

## CORD

Cast on 4 sts in yarn B on 4.5mm needles (UK 7, US 7) and knit in the round as foll: knit 4 sts, *slide sts to right end of needle, bring yarn round back of work and knit 4 sts*, rep from * to * until cord measures approx 110cm (43in). Cast (bind) off. Alternatively, use an i-cord maker or a French knitting machine.

Thread cord through casing on hood.

## MAKING UP

Graft or sew together at underarms.

Fold bottom edge of body over to WS and sew down loosely.

## CHART

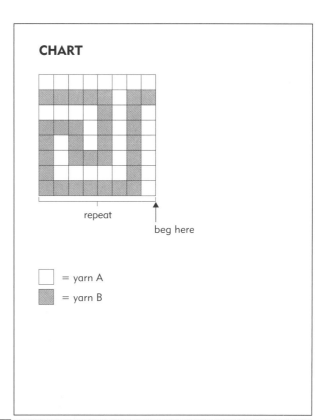

repeat

beg here

□ = yarn A

▨ = yarn B

# JOY SWEATER
## WOMEN

This beautiful sweater is a joy to wear. If it's a warm day, you can detach the separate cowl. It has beautiful cables and a flattering long shape, and can be turned into a long tunic if knitted longer. Joy also works well with the Viking (see page 132).

**YARN**
Gann Garn Sky (62% baby alpaca, 16% acrylic, 22% nylon, 50g (1¾oz) = approx 150m (164yd))

**DIFFICULTY**
Experienced

**SIZES**
XS(S:M:L:XL:XXL)
See garment measurements to check sizing

**GARMENT MEASUREMENTS**
Chest approx 90(100:110:120:130:140)cm (35½(39½:43¼:47¼:51:55¼)in)
Length approx 66(68:70:72:74:76)cm (26(26¾:27½:28¼:29¼:30)in)
Sleeve length approx 49(49:50:50:50:51)cm (19¼(19¼:19¾:19¾:19¾:20)in)

**YARN AMOUNT**
**Sweater:** 8(9:10:10:11:12) balls
**Cowl:** three balls for all sizes (see bottom-right photo on page 142 to see sweater without cowl)

**SHADES USED IN VERSIONS SHOWN**
Wine 608
(Alternative colourway: Light grey 606, page 142)

**SUGGESTED NEEDLES**
5mm (UK 6, US 8) and 6mm (UK 4, US 10) long and short circular needles and dpns. Change from long to short circular needle and to dpns as number of sts and diameter of work decreases and vice versa.

**TENSION (GAUGE)**
17 sts and 22 rounds to approx 10cm (4in) over stocking (stockinette) stitch using 6mm (UK 4, US 10) needles. Remember that you need to maintain an even tension for a successful result. Check your tension by knitting a test swatch. Count the number of stitches per 10cm (4in). If you have more stitches than stated, go up a needle size. If you have fewer stitches, switch to smaller needles.

**BACK**
Cast on 78(86:96:102:112:120) sts using 5mm (UK 6, US 8) circular needle. Work back and forth as foll:
Row 1 (RS): Knit.
Row 2 (WS): k1, p1.
Rep these 2 rows until work measures 10cm (4in).

**FRONT**
Cast on and work as for back.

## BODY

Place both pieces on the same 6mm (UK 4, US 10) circular needle. 156(172:192:204:224:240) sts. Place marker at each side. Cont in stocking (stockinette) stitch in the round until work measures approx 46(47:48:49:50:51)cm (18(18½:19:19¼:19¾:20)in). Cast (bind) off 10 sts on each side, 5 sts each side of marker. Divide and work front and back separately.

## BACK

Work back and forth in stocking (stockinette) stitch, at the same time casting (binding) off for armhole on each row as follows: 2, 2, 1, 1 sts. 56(64:74:80:90:98) sts. Cont until armhole measures approx 20(21:22:23:24:25)cm (7¾(8¼:8¾:9:9½:9¾)in) and whole work measures approx 66(68:70:72:74:76)cm (26(26¾:27½:28¼:29¼:30)in). Cast (bind) off.

## FRONT

Work back and forth and shape armhole as for back. When work measures approx 7cm (2¾in) before total length, cast (bind) off centre 18(18:20:20:22:22) sts. Work right and left side of neck separately and cont to decrease for neck at both sides on every alt row as follows: 3, 2, 1 sts. 13(17:21:24:28:32) sts rem for shoulder. Work until front is the same length as back. Cast (bind) off. Work other side of front in the same way.

## SLEEVES

Cast on 34(34:36:36:40:40) sts using 5mm (UK 6, US 8) dpns. Work 5cm (2in) in k1, p1 rib in the round. Change to 6mm (UK 4, US 10) dpns and knit 1 round increasing evenly across round to 64(66:70:72:74:78) sts. Cont as follows: work 16(17:19:20:21:23) sts in stocking (stockinette) stitch, then cable patt over 32 sts, then 16(17:19:20:21:23) sts in stocking (stockinette) stitch. Place marker at beg of round = centre underarm. Cont as set, at the same time increasing 1 st each side of marker approx every 4(4:4:4.4:4)cm (1½(1½:1½:1½:1½:1½)in) until there are 80(82:86:90:92:96) sts. Work until sleeve measures stated or desired length. Cast (bind) off 10 sts at centre underarm, 5 sts each side of marker. Cont back and forth and work sleeve head while continuing to work patt at centre sleeve as before. Cont as follows: dec 2 sts on alt rows twice for all sizes. Then dec 1 st on each

side on every alt row until armhole measures approx 12(13:14:15:16:17)cm (4¾(5:5½:6:6¼:6¾)in). Then dec 2 sts on every alt row on both sides three times in total. Finally, dec 1 st on every row, on RS and WS, six times on each side in total. Cast (bind) off rem sts straight. Work other sleeve the same way.

## MAKING UP

Graft or sew together at shoulders.

**Neckband:** Pick up or work 84(84:88:88:92:92) sts using 5mm (UK 6, US 8) circular needle. Work in in k1, p1 rib in the round until neckband measures approx 6cm (2½in). Cast (bind) off loosely. Fold neck edge over to WS and sew down loosely.

**Sew in sleeves:** Pin centre of sleeve head to centre of shoulder seam. Start by sewing cast (bound) off sts from centre underarm and body together. Then sew up each side. At top of sleeve head pleat excess sts and sew down.

## SEPARATE COWL

Cast on 74 sts using 6mm (UK 4, US 10) circular needle. Cont as follows: work 5 sts in k1, p1 rib, then work patt as shown in chart, repeating chart twice widthwise over 64 sts. End row with 5 sts in k1, p1 rib. Work back and forth as set until work measures approx 65cm (25½in). Cast (bind) off. Fold cowl in half and sew cast on edge to cast (bound) off edge.

## CHART

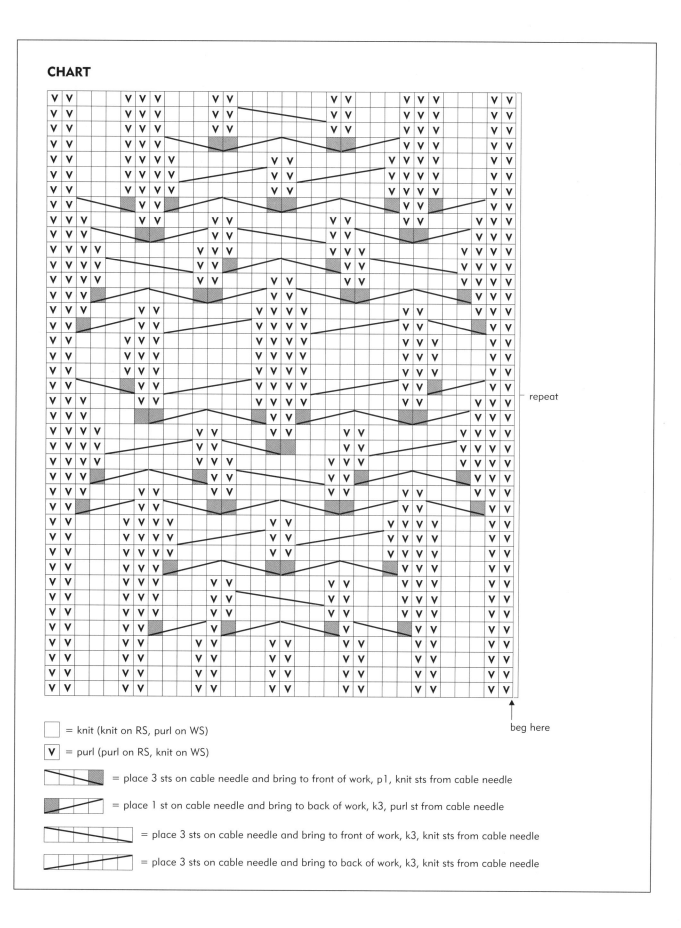

repeat

beg here

☐ = knit (knit on RS, purl on WS)

V = purl (purl on RS, knit on WS)

= place 3 sts on cable needle and bring to front of work, p1, knit sts from cable needle

= place 1 st on cable needle and bring to back of work, k3, purl st from cable needle

= place 3 sts on cable needle and bring to front of work, k3, knit sts from cable needle

= place 3 sts on cable needle and bring to back of work, k3, knit sts from cable needle

# JOY SWEATER
## CHILDREN

This lovely sweater is great for children too.

**YARN**
Gann Garn Sky (62% baby alpaca, 16% acrylic, 22% nylon, 50g (1¾oz) = approx 150m (164yd))

**DIFFICULTY**
Experienced

**SIZES**
Age 4(6:8:10:12)
See garment measurements below to check sizing

**GARMENT MEASUREMENTS**
Chest approx 65(70:75:80:85)cm
(25½(27½:29½31½:33½)in)
Length approx 50(54:58:62:68)cm
(19¾(21¼:22¾:24½:26¾)in)
Sleeve length approx 27(33:36:38:40)cm
(10¾(13:14¼:15:15¾)in)

**YARN AMOUNT**
**Sweater:** 4(5:6:7:7) balls
**Cowl:** two balls for all sizes (see top-right photo on page 147 to see sweater without cowl)

**SHADE USED IN VERSION SHOWN**
Light beige 605

**SUGGESTED NEEDLES**
5mm (UK 6, US 8) and 6mm (UK 4, US 10) long and short circular needles and dpns. Change from long to short circular needle and to dpns as number of sts and diameter of work decreases and vice versa.

**TENSION (GAUGE)**
17 sts and 22 rounds to approx 10cm (4in) over stocking (stockinette) stitch using 6mm (UK 4, US 10) needles. Remember that you need to maintain an even tension for a successful result. Check your tension by knitting a test swatch. Count the number of stitches per 10cm (4in). If you have more stitches than stated, go up a needle size. If you have fewer stitches, switch to smaller needles.

**BACK**
Cast on 56(60:64:68:72) sts using 5mm (UK 6, US 8) circular needle. Work back and forth as foll:
Row 1 (RS): knit.
Row 2 (WS): k1, p1.

Rep these 2 rows until work measures 8(8:8:8:10)cm (3¼(3¼:3¼:3¼:4)in).

**FRONT**
Cast on and work as for back.

## BODY

Place both pieces on the same 6mm (UK 4, US 10) circular needle. 112(120:128:136:144) rem sts. Place marker at each side. Cont in stocking (stockinette) stitch until work measures approx 36(39:42:45:50)cm (14¼(15¼:16½:17¾:19¾)in). If you want a longer or shorter tunic, adjust the length now. Cast (bind) off 6 sts on each side, 3 sts each side of marker. Work front and back separately.

## BACK

Cont back and forth in stocking (stockinette) stitch, at the same time casting (binding) off for armhole at each side on each row as follows: 2, 2, 1 sts. 40(44:48:52:56) rem sts. Cont until armhole measures approx 14(15:16:17:18)cm (5½(6:6¼:6¾:7)in) and whole work measures approx 50(54:58:62:68)cm (19¾(21¼:22¾:24½:26¾)in). Cast (bind) off or place sts on a holder.

## FRONT

Work back and forth and shape armhole as for back. When work measures approx 5(5:6:6:6)cm (2(2:2½:2½:2½)in) before total length, cast (bind) off the centre 10(10:12:14:16) sts. Work each side separately and cont to decrease for neck at both sides on every alt row as follows: 3, 2, 1 sts. 9(11:12:13:14) rem sts for shoulder. Work until front is the same length as back. Cast (bind) off or place sts on a holder. Work other side of front in the same way.

## SLEEVES

Cast on 26(28:30:32:34) sts using 5mm (UK 6, US 8) dpns. Work 4cm (1½in) in k1, p1 rib in the round. Change to 6mm (UK 4, US 10) needles and knit 1 round increasing evenly across round to 50(52:54:58:60) sts. Cont as follows: work 13(14:15:17:18) sts in stocking (stockinette) stitch, then cable patt over 24 sts, then 13(14:15:17:18) sts in stocking (stockinette) stitch. Place marker at beg of round for the centre underarm. Cont as set, at the same time increasing 1 st each side of marker approx every 3.5(4:4:4.5.4.5)cm (1⅜(1½:1½:1½:1¾:1¾)in) until there are 62(66:70:72:76) sts. Work until sleeve measures stated or desired length. Cast (bind) off 6 sts at centre underarm, 3 sts each side of marker. Cont back and forth and work sleeve head while continuing to work patt at centre sleeve as before. Cont as follows: dec 2 sts on alt rounds twice for all sizes. Then dec 1 st on each side on every alt row until armhole measures approx 7(8:9:10:11)cm (2¾(3¼:3½:4:4¼)in). Then dec 2 sts on alt rows on both sides twice in total. Finally, dec 1 st on every row, four times on each side in total. Note that you are now decreasing on RS and WS. Cast (bind) off rem sts straight. Work other sleeve the same way.

## MAKING UP

Graft or sew together at shoulders.

**Neckband:** Pick up or work 54(58:62:66:72) sts using 5mm (UK 6, US 8) circular needle. Work in the round in k1, p1 rib until neckband measures approx 6cm (2½in). Cast (bind) off loosely. Fold neck edge over to WS and sew down loosely.

**Sew in sleeves:** Pin centre of sleeve head to centre of shoulder seam. Beg by sewing cast (bound) off sts from centre underarm and body together. Then sew up each side. At top of sleeve head pleat excess sts and sew down.

## SEPARATE COWL

Cast on 58 sts using 6mm (UK 4, US 10) circular needle. Cont as follows: work 5 sts in k1, p1 rib, then work patt as shown in chart, repeating patt twice widthwise over 48 sts. Then work 5 sts in k1, p1 rib. Work back and forth as set until work measures approx 50(55:55:60:60)cm (19¾(21¾:21¾:23½:23½)in). Cast (bind) off. Fold collar in half and sew cast on edge to cast (bound) off edge, creating a cylinder.

## CHART

SLEEVE PATTERN – 24 sts

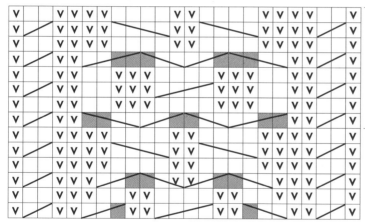

repeat

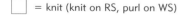 = knit (knit on RS, purl on WS)

 = purl (purl on RS, knit on WS)

= place 2 sts on cable needle and bring to front of work, p1, knit sts from cable needle

= place 1 st on cable needle and bring to back of work, k2, purl st from cable needle

= place 2 sts on cable needle and bring to front of work, k2, knit sts from cable needle

= place 2 sts on cable needle and bring to back of work, k2, knit sts from cable needle

= place 2 sts on cable needle and bring to front of work, p2, knit sts from cable needle

= place 2 sts on cable needle and bring to back of work, k2, purl sts from cable needle

= knit second st behind first st without taking sts off needle, k1, slip both sts off

# OCEAN WAVES SWEATER

This is a sweater for urban life and out at sea. The textured pattern is tough and elegant, and the boat neckline makes it light and airy.

## YARN
Gann Garn Tweed (80% wool, 20% polyamide, 50g (1¾oz) = approx 112m (122yd))

## DIFFICULTY
Beginner

## SIZES
S(M:L:XL:XXL:LASSE)
See garment measurements to check sizing

## GARMENT MEASUREMENTS
Chest approx 95(102:109:116:124:124)cm (37½(40¼:43:45½:48¾:48¾)in)
Length approx 66(68:70:72:74:76)cm (26(26¾:27½:28¼:29¼:30)in)
Sleeve length approx 50(50:52:52:53:53)cm (19¾(19¾:20½:20½:20¾:20¾)in)

## YARN AMOUNT
9(10:11:12:13:13) balls

## SHADE USED IN VERSION SHOWN
Petrol 907

## SUGGESTED NEEDLES
4mm (UK 8, US 6) and 5mm (UK 6, US 8) long and short circular needles and dpns. Change from long to short circular needle and to dpns as number of sts and diameter of work decreases and vice versa.

## TENSION (GAUGE)
17 sts and 24 rounds to approx 10cm (4in) over stocking (stockinette) stitch using 5mm (UK 6, US 8) needles. Remember that you need to maintain an even tension for a successful result. Check your tension by knitting a test swatch. Count the number of stitches per 10cm (4in). If you have more stitches than stated, go up a needle size. If you have fewer stitches, switch to smaller needles.

## GARTER STITCH ON CIRCULAR NEEDLE
1 ridge of garter stitch = 1 round knit, 1 round purl

**TIP:** Garter stitch has a tendency to be looser than stocking (stockinette) stitch so change to 4mm (UK 8, US 6) needles if necessary.

## BODY

This sweater is worked from the bottom up. Cast on 160(176:188:200:216:216) sts using 4mm (UK 8, US 6) circular needle. Work in k2, p2 rib until work measures approx 6cm (2½in) for all sizes. Change to 5mm (UK 6, US 8) circular needle. Place marker at each side, marking 80(88:94:100:108:108) sts each for front and back. Cont in the round, working garter stitch over 20 sts at each side, 10 sts each side of marker, and stocking (stockinette) stitch over rem sts. Work following chart until body measures approx 48(49:50: 51:52:54)cm (19(19¼:19¾:20:20½:21¼)in). Cast (bind) off 12 sts on each side, 6 sts each side of marker. Set work aside while you knit sleeves.

## SLEEVES

Cast on 36(36:40:40:44:44) sts using 4mm (UK 8, US 6) dpns. Work 6cm (2½in) in k2, p2 rib in the round. Change to 5mm (UK 6, US 8) needles. Knit 1 round increasing 8 sts evenly across round to 48(48:50:50:54:54) sts. Place marker at beg of round = centre underarm. Work in the round in stocking (stockinette) stitch while increasing 1 st on each side of marker approx every 3.5(3:3:2½:2½:2½)cm (1⅜(1¼:1¼:1:1:1)in). Cont until work measures stated or desired length and there are 62(64:68:72:74:74) sts in round. On last round, cast (bind) off 12 sts at centre underarm, 6 sts each side of marker. Set aside and work other sleeve the same way.

## YOKE

Place all pieces on the same 5mm (UK 6, US 8) circular needle with one sleeve positioned over each set of cast (bound) off sts on body. 236(256:276:296:316:316) sts. Knit one round decreasing evenly across all sts to 228(252:276:288:300:300) sts. Cont in patt following chart, decreasing as shown until there are 76(84:92:96:100:100) sts in round. End with 0(2:4:4:6:6) rounds in stocking (stockinette) stitch. Work neckband.

## NECKBAND

Change to 4mm (UK 8, US 6) circular needle and work 6 rounds in stocking (stockinette) stitch. Cast (bind) off. Allow edge to roll outwards.

## MAKING UP

Sew together at underarms. Weave in all loose ends on WS.

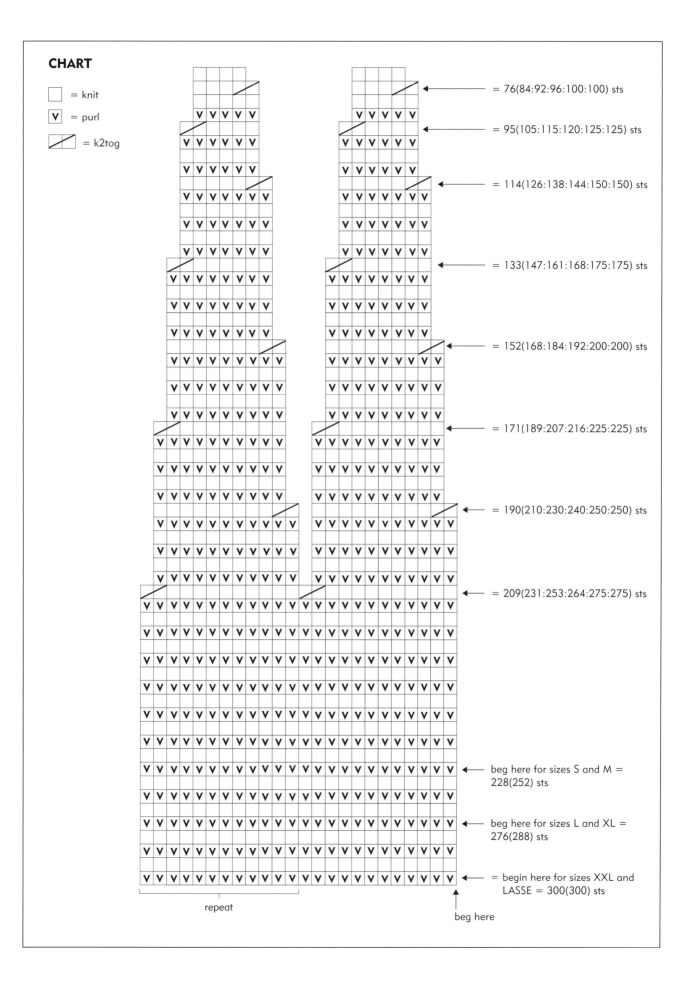

**CHART**

☐ = knit

**V** = purl

⟋ = k2tog

= 76(84:92:96:100:100) sts

= 95(105:115:120:125:125) sts

= 114(126:138:144:150:150) sts

= 133(147:161:168:175:175) sts

= 152(168:184:192:200:200) sts

= 171(189:207:216:225:225) sts

= 190(210:230:240:250:250) sts

= 209(231:253:264:275:275) sts

beg here for sizes S and M = 228(252) sts

beg here for sizes L and XL = 276(288) sts

= begin here for sizes XXL and LASSE = 300(300) sts

repeat

beg here

# THREE SWORDS SWEATER

This is a great-looking, classic sweater. The pattern is inspired by the majestic Viking monument, *Sver i fjell* ('Swords in Rock'), which celebrates the battle where Harald Fairhair united Norway. It can be knitted in a roomier size if you prefer.

## YARN
Gann Garn Sky (62% baby alpaca, 16% acrylic, 22% nylon, 50g (1¾oz) = approx 150m (164yd))

## DIFFICULTY
Intermediate

## SIZES
S(M:L:XL:XXL:LASSE)
See garment measurements below to check sizing

## GARMENT MEASUREMENTS
Chest approx 99(106:120:127:134:127)cm
(39(41¾:47¼:50:52¾:50)in)
Length approx 66(68:70:72:74:76)cm
(26(26¾:27½:28¼:29¼:30)in)
Sleeve length approx 50(50:52:52:53:53)cm
(19¾(19¾:20½:20½:20¾:20¾)in)

## YARN AMOUNT
Yarn A: 7(8:8:9:10:9) balls
Yarn B: 1(1:1:1:1:1) ball

## SHADES USED IN VERSION SHOWN
Yarn A: Grey melange 607
Yarn B: Natural 601

## SUGGESTED NEEDLES
5mm (UK 6, US 8) and 6mm (UK 4, US 10) long and short circular needles and dpns. Change from long to short circular needle and to dpns as number of sts and diameter of work decreases and vice versa.

> **TIP:** To ensure a good result when knitting with two or more colours, always hold yarns in the same position behind the work. Decide to keep the background colour innermost and the contrast colour outermost, for example.

## TENSION (GAUGE)
17 sts and 21 rounds to approx 10cm (4in) over stocking (stockinette) stitch using 6mm (UK 4, US 10) needles. Remember that you need to maintain an even tension for a successful result. Check your tension by knitting a test swatch. Count the number of stitches per 10cm (4in). If you have more stitches than stated, go up a needle size. If you have fewer stitches, switch to smaller needles.

> **TIP:** The tension will be tighter when working the Fair Isle pattern and it is often useful to go up 0.5mm or 1mm in needle size (one or two UK/US sizes).

**BODY**

Cast on 168(180:204:216:228:216) sts using 5mm (UK 6, US 8) circular needle and yarn A. Work k2, p2 rib in the round until rib measures 6cm (2½in) for all sizes. Change to 6mm (UK 4, US 10) circular needle. Place marker at each side, marking 85(91:103:109:115:109) sts for front and 83(89:101:107:113:107) sts for back. Work in stocking (stockinette) stitch in the round until work measures approx 46(47:48:49:50:51)cm (18(18½:19:19¼:19¾:20)in). Cast (bind) off 12 sts on each side, 6 sts each side of marker. Set work aside while you knit sleeves.

**SLEEVES**

Cast on 36(36:36:40:40:40) sts using 5mm (UK 6, US 8) dpns and yarn A. Work 6cm (2½in) in the round in rib as for bottom of body. Change to 6mm (UK 4, US 10) needles and knit 1 round increasing evenly across round to 47(49:53:55:57:59) sts. Place marker at beg of round = centre underarm. Work in the round in stocking (stockinette) stitch while increasing 1 st on each side of marker approx every 4.5(4:4:3.5:3.5:3.5)cm (1¾(1½:1½:1⅜:1⅜:1⅜)in) to a total 67(71:75:79:81:85) sts. Work until sleeve

measures stated or desired length. Cast (bind) off 12 sts at centre underarm, 6 sts each side of marker. Set work aside and work other sleeve the same way.

**YOKE**

Place all pieces on the same 6mm (UK 4, US 10) circular needle with one sleeve positioned over each set of cast (bound) off sts on body. 254(274:306:326:342:338) sts. Knit 1 round decreasing evenly across round to 252(264:300:324:336:336) sts. Work in the round in patt following chart. There are now 84(88:100:108:112:112) sts in round. Knit 1 round decreasing evenly across round to 84(88: 92:96:100:104) sts. Work neckband.

**NECKBAND**

Move rem sts to 5mm (UK 6, US 8) circular needle and use yarn A. Work in the round in k2, p2 rib until neckband measures approx 4cm (1½in). Purl 1 round (forms foldline). Work 4cm (1½in) in rib. Cast (bind) off loosely in rib. Fold neck edge over to WS and sew down loosely.

**MAKING UP**

Sew together at underarms. Weave in all loose ends on WS.

# CHART

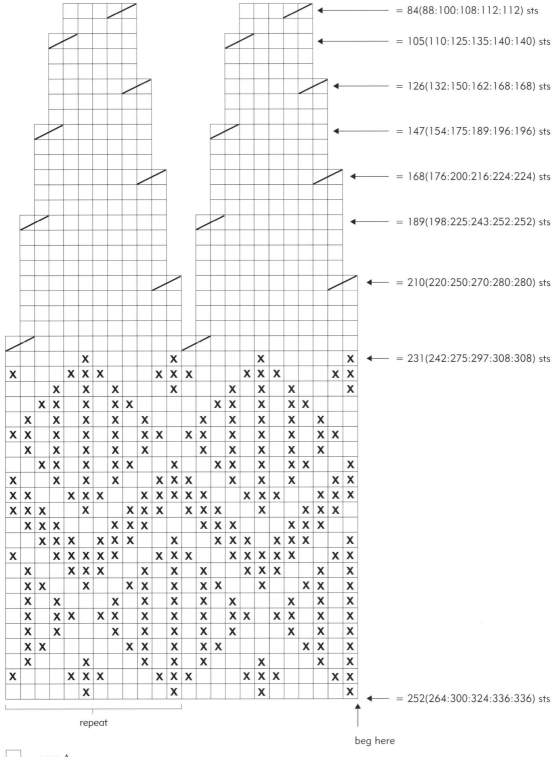

= 84(88:100:108:112:112) sts

= 105(110:125:135:140:140) sts

= 126(132:150:162:168:168) sts

= 147(154:175:189:196:196) sts

= 168(176:200:216:224:224) sts

= 189(198:225:243:252:252) sts

= 210(220:250:270:280:280) sts

= 231(242:275:297:308:308) sts

= 252(264:300:324:336:336) sts

repeat

beg here

☐ = yarn A

X = yarn B

╱ = k2tog

# GLIMA SWEATER

*Glima* was Viking wrestling, a friendly combat sport and test of strength. This sweater is great for sport and physical labour.

**YARN**
Gann Garn Tweed (80% wool, 20% polyamide, 50g (1¾oz) = approx 112m (122yd))

**DIFFICULTY**
Intermediate

**SIZES**
S(M:L:XL:XXL:LASSE)
See garment measurements to check sizing.

**GARMENT MEASUREMENTS**
Chest approx 95(102:109:116:124:124)cm
(37½:(40¼:43:45½:48¾:48¾)in)
Length approx 66(68:70:72:74:76)cm
(26(26¾:27½:28¼:29¼:30)in)
Sleeve length approx 50(50:52:52:53:53)cm
(19¾(19¾:20½:20½:20¾:20¾)in)

**YARN AMOUNT**
Yarn A: 10(11:12:13:14:14) balls
Yarn B: one ball for all sizes

**SHADES USED IN VERSION SHOWN**
Yarn A: Military green 904
Yarn B: Rust 903

**SUGGESTED NEEDLES**
4mm (UK 8, US 6) and 5mm (UK 6, US 8) long and short circular needles and dpns

**TENSION (GAUGE)**
17 sts and 22 rounds to approx 10cm (4in) over stocking (stockinette) stitch using 5mm (UK 6, US 8) needles. Remember that you need to maintain an even tension for a successful result. Check your tension by knitting a test swatch. Count the number of stitches per 10cm (4in). If you have more stitches than stated, go up a needle size. If you have fewer stitches, switch to smaller needles.

**BODY**
Cast on 160(176:188:200:216:216) sts using 4mm (UK 8, US 6) circular needle. Work in k2, p2 rib in the round until work measures approx 6cm (2½in) for all sizes. Change to 5mm (UK 6, US 8) circular needle. Place marker at each side, marking 80(88:94:100:108:108) sts each for front and back. Cont in stocking (stockinette) stitch in the round until work measures approx 48(49:50:51:53:54)cm (19(19¼:19¾:20:20¾:21¼)in). Cast (bind) off 12 sts on each side, 6 sts each side of marker. Set work aside while you knit sleeves.

## SLEEVES

Cast on 36(36:40:40:44:44) sts using 4mm (UK 8, US 6) dpns. Work 6cm (2½in) in k2, p2 rib in the round for all sizes. Change to 5mm (UK 6, US 8) needles. Knit 1 round increasing 8 sts evenly across round to 48(48:50:50:54:54) sts. Place marker at beg of round = centre underarm. Work in the round in stocking (stockinette) stitch while increasing 1 st on each side of marker approx every 6(5.5:5:4:4.5:4.5)cm (2½(2¼:2:1½:1¾:1¾)in). When work measures approx 41(41:43:43:44:44)cm (16¼(16¼:17:17:17¼:17¼)in), work patt: work to centre 16 sts in round, work stocking (stockinette) stitch over these 16 sts while increasing 8 sts. 24 sts rem in centre of round for patt. Work stocking (stockinette) stitch to end of round. On next round, beg patt as shown in chart over centre 24 sts with stocking (stockinette) stich on either side. Cont increases at centre underarm as before, making 7(8:9:11:10:10) increases in total. Once patt is complete, dec 8 sts across patt sts by k2tog equivalent to the increases. 16 patt sts rem. Work until sleeve measures stated or desired length. There should now be a total 62(64:68:72:74:74) sts on needles. On last round, cast (bind) off 12 sts at centre underarm, 6 sts each side of marker. Set work aside and work other sleeve the same way.

## YOKE

Place all pieces on the same 5mm (UK 6, US 8) circular needle with one sleeve positioned over each set of cast (bound) off sts on body. 236(256:276:296:316:316) rem sts. Place marker at each join. Cont in stocking (stockinette) stitch in the round, working decreases at all four joins. Beg round at back on right shoulder. Work until 3 sts before marker, sl1 loosely, k1, psso, k2, k2tog. 8 sts decreased in round. Dec in same way on every alt round until you have worked raglan decrease rounds 17(19:22:24:26:26) times in total. On next round, cast (bind) off centre 10(14:14:16:20:20) sts on front for neck.

Work to end of round. Break yarn and beg at front after cast (bound) off sts. Cont back and forth in stocking (stockinette) stitch and in patt as before. At the same time, cont to dec at each side of neck on alt rows as foll: 4, 2, 1 sts for all sizes. Cont until you have worked 21(23:26:28:30:30) raglan decreases on back in total. 44(44:40:42:42:42) rem sts. Work neckband.

## NECKBAND

Using 5mm circular needle (UK 6, US 8), pick up 28(32:36:36:38:38) sts at front neck. There are now approx 92(100:100:102:104:104) sts in total. Work 20cm (8in) in stocking (stockinette) stitch in the round. Change to 4mm (UK 8, US 6) circular needle and yarn B. Work 2 rounds in stocking (stockinette) stitch. Create opening for cord: place marker at centre front and place two more markers approx 3cm (1¼in) on each side of centre marker. Make a hole at each marker by working k2tog, yo. Work 2.5cm (1in) in stocking (stockinette) stitch. Cast (bind) off loosely. Fold edge in to WS and sew down below the holes, which will show on RS.

## I-CORD

Cast on 4 sts using 4 mm (UK 8, US 6) dpns and yarn B and work in the round as foll: k4, slide sts to opposite side of needle, bring yarn round back of work and k4 again. Rep until cord measures approx 90cm (35½in). Cast (bind) off. Attach a safety pin to the cord and push it into one hole at front neck, then push the cord through the casing and out of the other hole.

## MAKING UP

Sew together at underarms. Weave in all loose ends neatly on WS.

## CHART

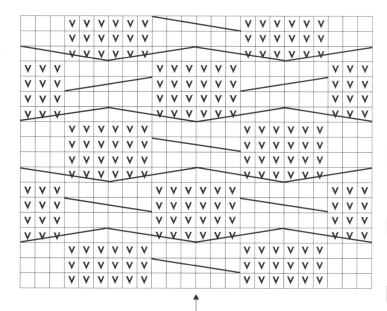

centre of sleeve

☐ = knit (knit on RS, purl on WS)

V = purl (purl on RS, knit on WS)

= place 3 sts on cable needle and bring to front of work, k3, knit sts from cable needle

= place 3 sts on cable needle and bring to back of work, k3, knit sts from cable needle

= place 3 sts on cable needle and bring to front of work, p3, knit sts from cable needle

= place 3 sts on cable needle and bring to back of work, k3, purl sts from cable needle

COSY
ACCESSORIES

# BRIOCHE SCARF

This toasty scarf is a great beginner project. If you like wrapping up warm in a big scarf, you can knit this pattern twice as long and wide.

## YARN
Gann Garn Sky (62% baby alpaca, 16% acrylic, 22% nylon, 50g (1¾oz) = approx 150m (164yd))

## DIFFICULTY
Beginner

## SIZE
Approximately 18 x 180cm (7 x 71in)

## YARN AMOUNT
Three balls

## SHADES USED IN VERSION SHOWN
Grey melange 607

## SUGGESTED NEEDLES
6mm circular needle (UK 4, US 10)

## TENSION (GAUGE)
13 sts to approx 10cm (4in) over brioche stitch using 6mm (UK 4, US 10) needles.
Remember that you need to maintain an even tension for a successful result. Check your tension by knitting a test swatch. Count the number of stitches per 10cm (4in). If you have more stitches than stated, go up a needle size. If you have fewer stitches, switch to smaller needles.

---

**BRIOCHE STITCH WORKED BACK AND FORTH**:
**Row 1 (RS):** k1 (edge st), *yo, sl1 loosely purlwise, knit yarn over and sl st from previous row together (this is the brioche st)*. Rep from * to * until last 2 sts. Yo, sl1 loosely purlwise, k1 (edge st).
**Row 2 (WS):** K1 (edge st), *knit yarn over and sl st from previous row together (this is the brioche st), sl1 loosely purlwise, k1*. Rep from * to * until last 2 sts. Work brioche st, k1 (edge st).

---

## SCARF
Using an elastic cast on, cast on 23 sts using 6mm (UK 4, US 10) circular needle. You can find instructions for how to knit an elastic cast on online.
**Set up row:** k1 (edge st), *k1, yo, sl1 loosely purlwise (these 2 loops will form brioche st on next round)*. Rep from * to * until last 2 sts, k1, k1 (edge st).
Cont in brioche stitch starting with row 1 as shown in box above, back and forth until scarf measures approx 180cm (70in) or desired length.
**Final row:** k1 (edge st), *p1, k1*. Rep from * to * until last 2 sts, k1, k1 (edge st).
Work elastic cast (bind) off (see below).

---

**ELASTIC CAST (BIND) OFF:**
**Knit sts:** yo knitwise, k1, slip yo and previous st over knit st.
**Purl sts:** yo purlwise, p1, slip yo and previous st over purl st.

---

# CUFFED HAT AND MITTENS
## FOR ADULTS AND CHILDREN

This gorgeous hat has matching mittens to go with it, and both are must-haves when you live in a tough climate like I do! Make both in all the colours of the rainbow, as they are easy first knits for beginners.

**YARN**
Gann Garn Sky (62% baby alpaca, 16% acrylic, 22% nylon, 50g (1¾oz) = approx 150m (164yd))

OR

Gann Garn Tweed (80% wool, 20% polyamide, 50g (1¾oz) = approx 112m (122yd))

**DIFFICULTY**
Beginner

**SIZES**
Age 2–4(6–8:10–12:women:men)
See garment measurements below to check sizing.

**GARMENT MEASUREMENTS**
Hat circumference approx 43(46:48:50:52)cm (17(18:19:19¾:20½)in)

**YARN AMOUNT**
2(2:2:3:3) balls

**SHADES USED IN VERSIONS SHOWN**
**Women's set:** Gann Garn Sky in Cognac 604 (opposite)
**Men's set:** Gann Garn Tweed in Grey Brown 911 (see page 167)

**SUGGESTED NEEDLES**
5mm (UK 6, US 8) and 6mm (UK 4, US 10) long and short circular needles and dpns

**TENSION (GAUGE)**
17 sts and 21 rounds to approx 10cm (4in) measured over stocking (stockinette) stitch using 6mm (UK 4, US 10) needles.
Remember that you need to maintain an even tension for a successful result. Check your tension by knitting a test swatch. Count the number of stitches per 10cm (4in). If you have more stitches than stated, go up a needle size. If you have fewer stitches, switch to smaller needles.

## HAT

Cast on 72(78:84:84:90) sts using 5mm (UK 6, US 8) circular needle. Work 10(10:12:12:12)cm (4(4:4¾:4¾:4¾)in) in k1, p1 rib in the round. The rib section will be folded double at the end and from now on the work will be measured from half the rib section (bottom of final hat). Change to 6mm (UK 4, US 10) circular needle and work in the round in stocking (stockinette) stitch. Cont until work measures approx 16(18:18:21:23)cm (6¼(7:7:8¼:9)in). Dec on every alt round by working k4, k2tog, repeated across whole round. Work 1 round without decreasing. On next decrease round, work k3, k2tog, repeated across whole round. Work in the same way with 1 fewer st between each decrease on every alt round until there are 12(13:14:14:15) sts in the round. Break yarn and pass through rem sts. Tighten and weave in yarn on WS. Attach a pompom to the top if desired.

## LEFT MITTEN

Cast on 30(34:34:36:38) sts using 5mm (UK 6, US 8) dpns. Work 10(10:12:12:12)cm (4(4:4¾:4¾:4¾)in) in k1, p1 rib in the round. The rib section will be folded double at the end and from now on the work will be measured from half the rib section (bottom of wrist). Change to 6mm (UK 4, US 10) needles and work approx 3(4:4:5:5)cm (1¼(1½:1½:2:2)in) in stocking (stockinette) stitch. Place marker at each side, marking 15(17:17:18:19) sts each front and back. Mark thumb opening as foll:
Beg from marker. Work 10(10:10:10:10) sts in stocking (stockinette) stitch, then work 4(6:6:7:8) sts in stocking (stockinette) stitch for thumb opening with waste yarn in a different colour. Then work rem 16(18:18:19:20) sts in stocking (stockinette) stitch. Cont in the round in stocking (stockinette) stitch over all stitches until mitten measures approx 15(17:20:22:24)cm (6:6¾:7¾:8¾:9½)in) measured from half of cuff, or until there are approx 3cm (1¼in) left before reaching final length. Try mitten on and work to desired length.

Dec at markers on each side: work until 2 sts before marker, sl1 loosely, k1, psso, k2tog.
Dec in this way on every alt round four times in total. Then dec on every round until there are 6(6:6:8:6) sts. Break yarn, thread it through rem sts, tighten yarn and weave in securely on WS.

## THUMB

Pull out the thread knitted over the 4(6:6:7:8) sts for thumb opening and place sts on a 6mm (UK 4, US 10) needle. Pick up an additional 6(8:8:9:10) sts round thumb opening. 10(14:14:16:18) sts. Work all these sts in stocking (stockinette) stitch in the round. Work until thumb measures approx 3.5(4:5:5.5:6)cm (1⅜(1½:2:2¼:2½), or until there is about 1cm (½in) left to final length. Try on mitten and knit thumb to desired length.
Now work k2, k2tog to decrease across whole round. 5(7:7:8:9) rem sts. Rep decrease round once more. 3(4:4:4:5) rem sts. Break yarn and pass through rem sts. Weave in yarn securely on WS.

## RIGHT MITTEN

Knit right mitten the same as the left mitten but with thumb on opposite side.

# REST-AND-SIT MAT

Half the fun of a long outdoor expedition is reaching the final destination: this mat will make sure you're comfy when you do. Everyone should have a mat like this in their backpack when out on a long trip; it's easy to knit too.

**YARN**
Gann Garn Sky (62% baby alpaca, 16% acrylic, 22% nylon, 50g (1¾oz) = approx 150m (164yd))

**DIFFICULTY**
Beginner

**SIZES**
Before felting approx 58 x 50cm (22¾ x 19¾in)
After felting approx 40 x 35cm (15¾ x 13¾in)

**YARN AMOUNT**
Three balls

**SHADES USED IN VERSION SHOWN**
Dark moss green 611

**SUGGESTED NEEDLES**
6mm circular needle (UK 4, US 10)

**TENSION (GAUGE)** 17 sts and 21 rounds to approx 21cm (8¼in) measured over garter stitch using 6mm (UK 4, US 10) needles.
Remember that you need to maintain an even tension for a successful result. Check your tension by knitting a test swatch. Count the number of stitches per 10cm (4in). If you have more stitches than stated, go up a needle size. If you have fewer stitches, switch to smaller needles.

---

**GARTER STITCH PATTERN:**
1 ridge of garter stitch =
knit 2 rows back and forth

---

**MAT**
Cast on 98 sts using 6mm (UK 4, US 10) circular needle. Work back and forth in garter stitch until work measures approx 50cm (19¾in) – see pattern above.

**Cast (bind) off:** k2, pass first st over second st, *k1, pass previous st over knit st = 1 st decreased*, rep from * to * to end of row. Break yarn and thread through last st.
Weave in ends.

**Felting**
Wash in a washing machine on a short cycle at 40 degrees Celcius (104 degrees Fahrenheit) using ordinary detergent.
Stretch mat to shape and dry flat.

## CHART

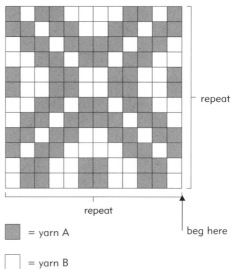

repeat

repeat

beg here

 = yarn A

= yarn B

**TIP:** To ensure a good result when knitting with two or more colours, always hold yarns in the same position behind the work. Decide to keep the background colour innermost and the contrast colour outermost, for example.

# BREEZE HAT
## FOR ADULTS AND CHILDREN

If you want a hat to match your sweater (see page 74), this warm hat in the same pattern as the Breeze sweater is just the thing.

**YARN**
Gann Garn Sky (62% baby alpaca, 16% acrylic, 22% nylon, 50g (1¾oz) = approx 150m (164yd))

**DIFFICULTY**
Intermediate

**SIZES**
Age 2–4(6–8:10–12:women:men)

**GARMENT MEASUREMENTS**
Hat circumference approx 42(42:47:49:52)cm (16½(16½:18½:19¼:20½)in)

**YARN AMOUNT**
Yarn A: one ball for all sizes
Yarn B: one ball for all size

**SHADES USED IN VERSION SHOWN**
Yarn A: Grey melange 607
Yarn B: Natural 601

**SUGGESTED NEEDLES**
5mm (UK 6, US 8) and 6mm (UK 4, US 10) long and short circular needles and dpns

**TENSION (GAUGE)**
19 sts and 19 rounds to approx 10cm (4in) over pattern using 6mm (UK 4, US 10) needles. Remember that you need to maintain an even tension for a successful result. Check your tension by knitting a test swatch. Count the number of stitches per 10cm (4in). If you have more stitches than stated, go up a needle size. If you have fewer stitches, switch to smaller needles.

**HAT**
Cast on 80(80:90:90:100) sts using 5mm (UK 6, US 8) circular needle and yarn A. Work 10(10:12:12:12)cm (4(4:4¾:4¾:4¾)in) in k1, p1 rib in the round. Change to 6mm (UK 4, US 10) circular needle. Knit 1 round increasing evenly across round to 84(84:96:96:108) sts. Work in the round in stocking (stockinette) stitch following patt as shown in chart. Cont until work measures approx 17(18:19:21:23)cm (6¾(7:7½:8¼: 9)in). Then cont in stocking (stockinette) stitch using yarn A with no patt. Dec on every alt round by working k4, k2tog, repeated across whole round. Work 1 round without decreasing. On next round, work k3, k2tog, repeated across whole round. Work in the same way with 1 fewer st between each decrease on every alt round until there are 14(14:16:16:18) sts in the round. Break yarn and pass through rem sts. Tighten yarn and weave in securely on WS. Make a pompom and attach to the top if desired.

# SAILOR HAT

A tough hat for a tough sailor.

**YARN**
Gann Garn Myk Merino (100% superwash merino wool, 50g (1¾oz) = approx 120m (131yd))

**DIFFICULTY**
Intermediate

**SIZE**
One size

**SHADES USED IN VERSION SHOWN**
Yarn A: Slate 707
Yarn B: Light grey 706

**YARN AMOUNT**
Yarn A: two balls
Yarn B: one ball

**SUGGESTED NEEDLES**
3.5mm (UK 9/10, US 4) and 4mm (UK 8, US 6) circular needle and dpns

**TENSION (GAUGE)**
26 sts and 32 rounds to approx 10cm (4in) over rib using 4mm (UK 8, US 6) needles.
Maintain an even tension for a successful result. Check tension by knitting a test swatch. Count the stitches per 10cm (4in). If you have more stitches, go up a needle size. If you have fewer stitches, switch to smaller needles.

**HAT**
Cast on 120 sts using 4mm (UK 8, US 6) needles and yarn A. Work 6cm (2½in) in k3, p1 rib in striped patt (see page 68).

Turn work WS out. Work approx 21cm (8¼in) using yarn A in patt as shown in chart. See chart for where to start the round.
**Dec for top:** beg at round 1 or round 3 of chart, *p1, k2tog, k1*, rep from * to * to end of round (90 sts). Work 2 rounds in p1, k2 rib.
**Next round:** *p1, k2tog*, rep from * to * to end of round (60 sts).
Work 2 rounds in p1, k1 rib.
**Next round:** k2tog all the way round (30 sts). Knit 1 round.
**Next round:** k2tog all the way round (15 sts).
Break yarn, thread yarn through sts and secure firmly on WS.
Turn striped edge up towards RS.

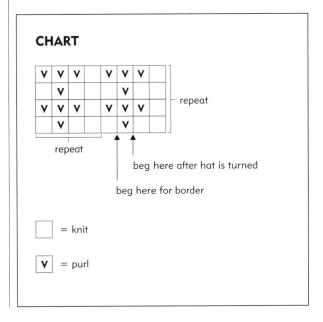

**CHART**

repeat

beg here after hat is turned

beg here for border

repeat

☐ = knit

V = purl

# SAILOR HAT
## CHILDREN

**YARN**
Gann Garn Myk Merino (100% superwash
merino wool, 50g (1¾oz) = approx 120m (131yd))

**DIFFICULTY**
Intermediate

**SIZES**
Age 2–4(6–8:10–12)

**YARN AMOUNT**
Yarn A: 1(2:2) balls
Yarn B: one ball for all sizes

**SHADES USED IN VERSION SHOWN**
Yarn A: Blue 714
Yarn B: Caramel 704

**SUGGESTED NEEDLES**
4mm (UK 8, US 6) and 4.5mm (UK 7, US 7) long and
short circular needles and dpns

**DECORATIONS FOR HAT**
One pompom (using yarn B), approx 6(7:8)cm
(2½(2¾:3¼)in) in diameter

**TENSION (GAUGE)**
25 sts and 32 rounds to approx 10cm (4in) measured
over pattern using 4.5mm (UK 7, US 7) needles.
Remember that you need to maintain an even
tension for a successful result. Check your tension by
knitting a test swatch. Count the number of stitches
per 10cm (4in). If you have more stitches than stated,
go up a needle size. If you have fewer stitches, switch
to smaller needles.

**STRIPED PATTERN:**
Work *1 round using yarn A, 1 round using
yarn B*, rep from * to * ending with 1 round
using yarn B. Cast on round counts as round 1.

**HAT**
Cast on 100(108:116) sts using 4.5mm (UK 7, US 7)
needles and yarn A. Work 4(5:5)cm (1½(2:2)in) in k3,
p1 rib in striped patt. Turn work WS out. Work approx
17(18:19)cm (6¾(7:7½)in) in patt following chart.
**Dec for top:** *k2tog, k1, p1*, rep from * to * to end of
round (75(81:87) sts). Work 2 rounds in k2, p1 rib.
**Next round:** *k2tog, p1*, rep from * to * to end of
round (50(54:58) sts). Work 2 rounds in k1, p1 rib.
**Next round:** k2tog all the way round (25(27:29) sts).
Knit 1 round.
**Next round:** k2tog all the way round. 13(14:15) sts.
Break yarn, thread yarn through sts and secure firmly
on WS. Fold edge with striped patt over to RS.
Make a pompom (using yarn B) approx 6(7:8)cm
(2½(2¾:3¼)in) in diameter. Sew pompom to top
of hat.

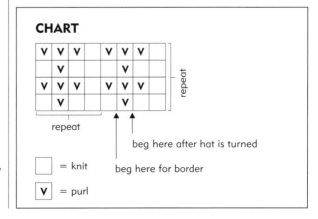

= knit

= purl

# SAGA HAT
## FOR ADULTS AND CHILDREN

A warm hat to match the Saga Sweater (see page 86).

**YARN**
Gann Garn Myk Merino (100% superwash
 merino wool, 50g (1¾oz) = approx 120m (131yd))

**DIFFICULTY**
Intermediate

**SIZES**
Age 2–4(6–8:10–12:women:men)

**GARMENT MEASUREMENTS**
Hat circumference approx 43(46:48:50:52)cm
(17(18:19:19¾:20½)in)

**YARN AMOUNT**
Yarn A: 1(1:1:2:2) balls
Yarn B: one ball for all sizes

**SHADES USED IN VERSION SHOWN**
Yarn A: Slate 707
Yarn B: Natural 701

**SUGGESTED NEEDLES**
3.5mm (UK 9/10, US 4) and 4mm (UK 8, US 6)
circular needles and 4mm (UK 8, US 6) dpns

**TENSION (GAUGE)**
24 sts and 28 rounds to approx 10cm (4in) over stocking
(stockinette) stitch using 4mm (UK 8, US 6) needles.
Remember that you need to maintain an even tension
for a successful result. Check your tension by knitting
a test swatch. Count the number of stitches per 10cm
(4in). If you have more stitches than stated, go up
a needle size. If you have fewer stitches, switch to
smaller needles.

> **TIP:** The tension will be tighter when working
> the Fair Isle pattern and it is often useful to go
> up 0.5mm or 1mm in needle size (one or two
> UK/US sizes).

## HAT

Cast on 96(100:108:116:120) sts using 3.5mm (UK 9/10, US 4) circular needle and yarn A. Work k2, p2 rib in striped patt as foll: *work 1(1:1:2:3) rounds using yarn A, 1(1:1:2:3) rounds using yarn B*. Cast on counts as round 1. Rep from * to * until rib measures approx 4(4:5:5:6)cm (1½(1½:2:2:2½)in) and end with 1 round using yarn B. Change to yarn A. Work approx 3(4:5:5:6)cm (1¼(1½:2:2:2½)in) in k2, p2 rib.

Change to 4mm (UK 8, US 6) circular needle. Cont in patt following chart. At the same time, on round 2, inc evenly across round to 102(108:114:120:126) sts.

Cont until patt section measures approx 14(16:18:20:22)cm (5½(6¼:7:7¾:8¾)in).

Change to yarn A, *k4, k2tog*, rep from * to * to end of round. Work 1 round without decreasing. On next round *k3, k2tog*, rep from * to * to end of round. Rep decreases on every alt round with 1 fewer st between each decrease on every alt round until there are 34(36:38:40:42) sts in the round. K2, k2tog until 17(18:19:19:20) rem sts in the round. Break yarn and pass through rem sts. Tighten and weave in yarn on WS.

Make a pompom (using yarn 2) approx 6(6:6:8)cm (2½(2½:2½:3¼)in) in diameter for the children's and women's hats.

Stitch pompom to top of hat.

Turn rib up to RS.

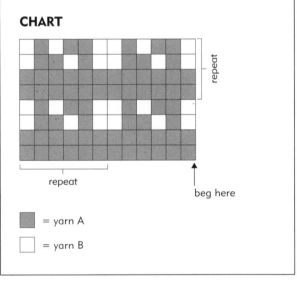

**CHART**

repeat

repeat

beg here

■ = yarn A

□ = yarn B

# SAGA MAT

Hats and gloves always get used, and so do mats to sit on!
They make great gifts for all the family, too. You can make
this mat from left-over yarn.

**YARN**
Gann Garn Sky (62% baby alpaca, 16% acrylic,
22% nylon, 50g (1¾oz) = approx 150m (164yd))

**DIFFICULTY**
Intermediate

**SIZES**
Before felting approx 58 x 50cm (22¾ x 19¾in)
After felting approx 40 x 35cm (15¾ x 13¾in)

**YARN AMOUNT**
Yarn A: two balls
Yarn B: one ball

**SHADES USED IN VERSION SHOWN**
Yarn A: Cognac 604
Yarn B: Light beige 605
(Alternative colourway: Grey 607, White 600, page 182)

**SUGGESTED NEEDLES**
6mm circular needle (UK 4, US 10)

**TENSION (GAUGE)**
17 sts and 21 rounds to approx 10cm (4in) over stocking
(stockinette) stitch using 6mm (UK 4, US 10) needles.
Remember that you need to maintain an even tension
for a successful result. Check your tension by knitting
a test swatch. Count the number of stitches per 10cm
(4in). If you have more stitches than stated, go up
a needle size. If you have fewer stitches, switch to
smaller needles.

**TIP:** The tension will be tighter when working
the Fair Isle pattern and it is often useful to go
up 0.5mm or 1mm in needle size (one or two
UK/US sizes).

## MAT

Cast on 98 sts using 6mm (UK 4, US 10) circular needle and yarn A.

Work back and forth in rib as foll:

**Row 1 (RS):** knit.

**Row 2 (WS):** *k1, p1*, rep from * to * to end of row.

Rep these 2 rows until work measures 5cm (2in). Beg on RS, work 10 sts in rib patt. This is the right edge. Work chart over 78 sts and 10 sts in rib patt for left edge. Cont as set until whole piece measures approx 45cm (17¾in). End with 2 rows using yarn A as shown in chart. Work 5cm (2in) in rib patt across all sts. Cast (bind) off.

## FELTING

Wash in a washing machine on a short cycle at 40 degrees Celcius (104 degrees Fahrenheit) using ordinary detergent.

Stretch the mat to shape and dry flat.

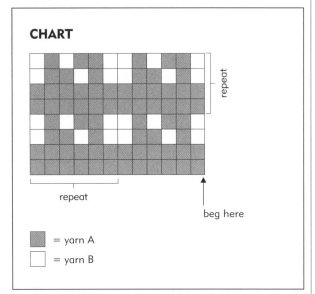

**CHART**

repeat

repeat

beg here

= yarn A

= yarn B

# SCARF IN THE ROUND

A stylish scarf that can be knitted longer if you like.

**YARN**
Gann Garn Myk Merino (100% superwash merino wool, 50g (1¾oz) = approx 120m (131yd))

**DIFFICULTY**
Beginner

**SIZES**
Child(women:men)

**YARN AMOUNT**
5(6:7) balls

**SHADES USED IN VERSION SHOWN**
Slate 707

**SUGGESTED NEEDLES**
Small 4mm (UK 8, US 6) circular needle

**TENSION (GAUGE)**
24 sts and 28 rounds to approx 10cm (4in) over stocking (stockinette) stitch using 4mm (UK 8, US 6) needles. Remember that you need to maintain an even tension for a successful result. Check your tension by knitting a test swatch. Count the number of stitches per 10cm (4in). If you have more stitches than stated, go up a needle size. If you have fewer stitches, switch to smaller needles.

**SCARF**
Cast on 62(72:82) sts using 4mm (UK 8, US 6) circular needle.
Work in stocking (stockinette) stitch in the round until work measures approx 140(160:170)cm (55(63:67)in) or desired length.
Cast (bind) off.
Lay flat and graft or sew each end together.
Dampen slightly with a damp cloth to make the foldlines sharper.

# DOUBLE-BRIMMED HAT
## FOR ADULTS AND CHILDREN

A perfectly beautiful hat.

**YARN**
Gann Garn Myk Merino (100% superwash
merino wool, 50g (1¾oz) = approx 120m (131yd))

**DIFFICULTY**
Beginner

**SIZES**
Age 2–4(6–8:10–12:women:men)

**YARN AMOUNT**
2(2:2:3:3) balls

**SHADES USED IN VERSION SHOWN**
Natural 701
(Alternative colourway: Slate 707, page 184)

**SUGGESTED NEEDLES**
4mm (UK 8, US 6) circular needles and dpns

**TENSION (GAUGE)**
24 sts and 28 rounds to approx 10cm (4in) over stocking
(stockinette) stitch using 4mm (UK 8, US 6) needles.
Remember that you need to maintain an even
tension for a successful result. Check your tension by
knitting a test swatch. Count the number of stitches
per 10cm (4in). If you have more stitches than stated,
go up a needle size. If you have fewer stitches, switch
to smaller needles.

**HAT**
Cast on 92(96:100:108:120) sts using 4mm (UK 8,
US 6) circular needle.
Work 9(13:17:21:23)cm (3½(5:6¾:8¼:9)in) stocking
(stockinette) stitch in the round. At the same
time, on last round dec 4 sts evenly across round.
88(92:96:104:112) sts. This row forms the foldline.
Turn work WS out.
Cont with 'hat section' and measure from here from
now on.
Work 12(13:14:16:17)cm (4¾(5:5½:6¼:6¾)in) in
stocking (stockinette) stitch. This side will turn
outwards.
Work is now a long tube with the WS facing outwards
on brim part of hat.
Place four markers with 22(23:24:26:28) sts between
each marker.
Dec for top: k2togTBL before each marker and
k2tog after each marker. 8 sts decreased on round.
Rep decreases on every alt round 6(9:10:11:12)
times in total, then on every round 4(1:1:1:1) times.
8(12:8:8:8) rem sts.
Break off yarn, pass it through sts and fasten on WS.

**Making up**
Fold the first 3.5(5.5:7.5:9.5:10.5)cm (1⅜(2¼:3:3¾:
4¼)in) to RS and sew with loose sts approx 2cm (¾in)
below where the 'hat section' begins. Fold the double
brim to RS once more. Only the stocking (stockinette)
stitch part of the hat will now be visible.
Dampen slightly with a cloth to sharpen the foldlines.